STUMBLE

• • •

The figure of the crucified invalidates
all thought which takes success for its standard.
—*Dietrich Bonhoeffer,* Ethics

The operation of the Church is entirely set up for the sinner,
which creates much misunderstanding among the smug.
—*Flannery O'Connor, letter to "A.", August 9, 1955*

Healthy people don't need a doctor—sick people do.
—*See Mark 2:17, Matthew 9:12, Luke 5:31*

• • •

STUMBLE

• • •

Virtue, Vice,
and the
Space Between

• • •

Heather King

Franciscan
MEDIA
Cincinnati, Ohio

Scripture passages have been taken from *New Revised Standard Version Bible*, copyright ©1989 by the Division of Christian Education of the National Council of the Churches of Christ in the U.S.A., and used by permission. All rights reserved.

Cover and book design by Mark Sullivan
Cover image © iStock | Enrico Fianchini
Back cover image © Jay Mantri

LIBRARY OF CONGRESS CATALOGING-IN-PUBLICATION DATA
King, Heather, 1952-
Stumble : virtue, vice, and the space between / Heather King.
pages cm
Includes bibliographical references.
ISBN 978-1-61636-814-2 (alk. paper)
1. Christian life—Catholic authors. 2. Virtues. 3. Vices. I. Title.
BX2350.3.K55 2015
248.4'82—dc23
2014038033

ISBN 978-1-61636-814-2

Published by Franciscan Media
28 W. Liberty St.
Cincinnati, OH 45202
www.FranciscanMedia.org

Printed in the United States of America.
Printed on acid-free paper.
15 16 17 18 19 5 4 3 2 1

• • •

For Fern, Swallow, and Warren—
who go with me

• • •

Contents

Foreword

Listen, my friends, we have all read forewords that are fluffy or pompous or inane or insipid or pap or mere lists of the ingredients in the text to come. I refuse to write that sort of piece for Heather King, because Heather King is the most honest blistering succinct emotionally naked blunt writer in headlong bruised pursuit of the holiness of Everything That Is that I know, and I am an ink-junkie who reads ravenously looking for writers that tell it real, that say real things with passion and humor and a healthy dose of raw humility.

If this was another kind of foreword I would use interesting prickly words here like *alcoholic* and *barfly* and *divorced* and *breast cancer* and you would conjure up a certain idea of the terrific essayist Heather King. And you would be right, I guess, for all those words are true enough about Heather. But you would also be utterly totally completely wrong, because all those words are not definitions of the terrific honest observer and storyteller Heather King; they are places she has been, parts of her, but there is a roaring urge for witness in Heather's work that makes all those interesting, thorny words mere signposts along her tumultuous road.

Why should you read this book? Because Heather King writes the kind of sizzling, tart prose that Flannery O'Connor did. Heather King keeps trying to punch through the mere religiosity of Catholicism, and get down to the wild illogical unreasonable nonsensical furious genius of it, like Andre Dubus did. Heather

King, like J.F. Powers and Ron Hansen and Alice McDermott, hands you bruised people trying with all their motley might to listen to the revolutionary message of the Christ and live by its awful implications.

Heather King would be an unforgettable character in a glorious novel by Mary Gordon about a brave wisp of a woman trying, against all sense and reason, to witness the One in every moment, and to live in the ferocious flame of the Love, and hold fast to hope and mercy in a world of blood and rape, except that Heather King is real, and in the ancient tradition of the essay she uses herself as reporter, as wick, as prism, as muddled guide through the dimness between us and the Coherent Mercy.

Why should you read this book? Because there are pieces and passages in here you will never forget, and they are brutally honest, and funny, and searing, and they will remind you that we are all on the suffering road, holding hands as best we can.

Also I think that if you, like me, have the slightest belief, deep in your bones and way past sense and reason, that there *is* a roaring Love, that there *is* a vast Mercy, that there *is* an inexplicable Imagination that breathed everything into being and set the stars to spin in the void, that there *is* a Force filled with fire and unquench-able tenderness, that the gaunt Jewish mystic who walked this dust two thousand years ago told no lies and Love *is* the law, then you should read this book, and then go read the rest of Heather's essays. They are not only fine pieces of prose carpentry; that's an easy compliment. The bigger and better compliment is that they are some sort of naked artless prayer, stories of a desperate brave relentless search for ways to crack the ego and walk into the light, to shed masks and disguises and habits and greed, and reach, shaking with fear and awe, for the miraculous Love every-where available, if only we can find the humility and imagination and cheerful defiant courage to see it and sing it.

Which Heather does, in tart and wonderful ways. See for yourself.

—Brian Doyle, author of *The Thorny Grace of It*

INTRODUCTION

Redemption is not about being good, but about coming
fully alive.

Converting to Catholicism was the last thing I ever thought I'd do,
and yet, eighteen years after the fact, it seems almost inevitable.
I'd hungered and thirsted all my life: for answers, for meaning,
for love. And though I had never thought of myself as religious,
religious—which comes from the Latin *religare*, "to bind back;
to reconnect"—is exactly what I was. I was on a search, however
misguided, to connect with something deeper than myself. I
hungered for some Eden it seemed I'd lost before I ever found it.

When I washed up on the shore of the Church, I was newly
sober and didn't know how to live; I was scared of everybody and
everything. As an active alcoholic, I'd slavered over my morning
beers with the single-minded devotion of the faithful; slept around
with abandon; succumbed to blackouts that were echoes, however
crude, of the merging-with-God oblivion of the contemplative
mystics. I wanted to redeem myself. I wanted to be good.

That first time I walked into St. Basil's up on Wilshire Boulevard
in L.A., I thought cringingly, *Am I even allowed in here? Will they
kick me out because I'm not Catholic?* Then I saw Christ on the
cross above the altar, and all my doubts disappeared. Not because
I thought he had died for my sins, but because all the trappings
were stripped away to reveal a vulnerable human being, and I was

moved with pity for him. I saw that he understood my suffering and was with me. He made me see that I wasn't a product that needed to be improved, as the relentless culture of advertising told me, but a human being with a soul; that redemption wasn't as much about being good as about coming fully alive.

When I was a child, my mother saw to it that I attended Sunday school and was baptized in the Congregational Church, but I wasn't the least bit interested. Coming of age in the sixties, I had no conception of God and no desire for one. After reading Jean Paul Sartre's *No Exit* as a freshman in high school, I adopted the phrase "Hell is other people" as my personal creed. I should have looked in the mirror, for the twenty-year bout of alcoholism that followed—coupled with the irresponsibility, the sexual license, and the loss of moral values alcoholism engendered—was as close to hell as I ever want to get.

Somehow during this period I attended both college and law school. This might sound good on paper, but getting good marks in class and functioning in the world are two entirely different things. At the age of thirty-three, sick, demoralized, and thoroughly beaten down, I responded to the intervention my family had for me. I finally turned to other recovering alcoholics for help, and I stopped drinking. My "career" had never moved beyond waitressing, and though writing was the only occupation to which I felt drawn, in the sober light of day I saw the desire as an indulgence, a child's pipe dream.

Ever since I'd applied to law school, nothing had terrified me more than the prospect of actually working as an attorney. Nevertheless, two years sober and newly married, I moved from Boston to L.A. and found a job in a downtown law firm whose affairs were in a state of such stupendous disarray that I didn't take a lunch break for the first six months. I carried with me always the secret of my alcoholism and the fear that it had rendered me unfit for normal life. Why couldn't I be more grateful? Why couldn't I fit in like everyone else? This job was killing my soul, but I had so little sense of myself and so little awareness that the world offered many more possibilities than this one job, that I literally did not think I was allowed to quit.

Meanwhile, soon after I'd quit drinking, I'd embarked on a vaguely defined spiritual journey. I went through a long beginning stage in which I thought everything about the world was wrong. Now, having dimly grasped the concept of humility—and, naturally, taken it to its furthest, most unbalanced extreme—I thought everything about me was wrong. I was so devoid of theological grounding I wasn't even sure of the difference between the Old and New Testaments. In desperation I started reading random books about Christianity, by authors as diverse as Dietrich Bonhoeffer and Meister Eckhart, Romano Guardini and C.S. Lewis, St. Thérèse of Lisieux, and Thomas Merton.

I even, bit by bit, read the Gospels. Ever since my childhood stint in Sunday school, I had thought of the Gospels as stories about ancient men in dusty tunics. What struck me now, though, was how precisely the Gospels spoke to my own situation. For example, they began to explain why I was so deeply miserable in the legal profession: The Gospels talked about giving, while the basic premise of the law is hoarding. The Gospels talked about letting go, while the law advocated hanging on for all you were worth. The Gospels said to lay down your arms, and in law all we ever did was gird ourselves for battle.

I began going to Mass regularly and attending adult confirmation classes. I continued reading the Gospels, and their many layers of meaning went on applying directly to my life. "Lord, I am not worthy that you should enter under my roof," we Catholics pray, "but only say the word and my soul shall be healed." That's the beauty of it: We're not worthy, but we get invited to the feast anyway. If we had to be worthy, we'd spend all our time trying to convince ourselves and others of our worthiness. This way it's settled: You're welcome the way you are—half-assed, easily distracted, generally second-rate. But at least you've shown up, and we're not much better, so come on in and get yourself a plate.

My heart has been turned, more than once, from stone to flesh, because I've been forgiven and I've forgiven others; because for a drunk to get sober is more miraculous than the moving of any mountain. I believe that Christ is the Way, the Truth, and the Life because my experience has been that the bread of our daily lives—the least remarkable of our experiences, the least among us, the least loveable, least understandable parts of ourselves—seems to be exactly where we are most likely to meet God.

Jesus consented to live most of his adult life in obscurity, doing the grinding, anonymous work of coming fully, spiritually awake, and then he proceeded to live with total integrity, knowing full well that the religious and secular powers would eventually band together and kill him for it. He was focused on ultimate things every second of his life, which was why he got exasperated at his disciples, drove the moneychangers from the Temple, told the Pharisees, "You're worried about putting unclean things in from the outside, I'm worried about what's unclean on the inside." Moving a mountain is nothing, he said; the real miracles take place when we forgive, when we're honest.

He loved the lilies of the field and the mustard seed that grew into a bush so large that the birds of the air could nest in its branches; he loved fish grilled over an open fire and good simple bread. He said, "You have to be willing to endure awkwardness, uncertainty, and pain. You have to love God above all else. That's the way the universe is ordered. That's the only way your joy will be complete."

Chapter | One

COMPASSION

··

The Closest to Love We Ever Get

There is another world, and it is this one.[1]

—PAUL ELUARD

I'm a person who craves quiet and solitude, yet I lived in the crowded, noisy Los Angeles neighborhood of Koreatown for eighteen years. In 2010, I moved to another part of L.A. But back then, I told myself I lived in K'town because I had a spacious, beautiful apartment and a gated courtyard filled with hibiscus and pomegranates. I told myself it was because I paid only $760 a month in rent—half as much as almost anywhere else in the city.

But the longer I stayed, the more I saw it was not just the apartment that kept me there: it was the challenges, the dilemmas, the paradoxes. People blasted ranchera music at three in the morning but they also pruned bougainvillea into glories of cascading blooms. They spray-painted gang slogans on my garage door by night and scrubbed the sidewalks clean by day. As I hung out my clothes on the line by the lemon tree, my back was to a busted washing machine; across the alley, a brand new down comforter, still in its package, sat on top of a dumpster.

Part of my impulse in living there was to hide out from the rest of the city—from the mansions and Mercedes, the hipsters, the people writing screenplays in too-cool-to-care coffeehouses. In Koreatown I could hide from the glamour and glitz of L.A.—but

I could not hide out from myself. Here, every day, I would come face to face with the cross of my irritation, my anger, my racism, my fear. Here I was plunged into the deepest contradictions: between abundance and scarcity, community and solitude, sin and grace, my longing for wholeness and my resistance to it.

Here I had no voice, no particular power. At Mass at St. Basil's, at 24-Hour Fitness, at Charlie Chan's Printing, at Ralph's Grocery, at the Vietnamese shop where I got my pedicures, I was often the only white person present. When I called out my window to Jung, the kid next door, to keep it down, he yelled back, "We were here first! Why don't you move?" His nine-year-old face would be contorted by hate, while hurt and fury rose in my own throat. I didn't have to read the headlines on Iraq to know how wars start, how the battle lines are drawn.

I would drive from Koreatown to Death Valley, to Anza Borrego, to the East Mojave. Then, as now, I was pulled to the desert as if by a magnet; I was forever scheming to escape there for a week, or two, or a month. I devoured books about the desert, and yet I was uneasy with the "nature" writers who left out human beings, who saw us as a blight on the landscape.

Living in Koreatown fortified my sense of apartness. It allowed me to be in the city but not always of it; it shaped me as a writer. But a writer has to be fully engaged: emotionally, spiritually, physically; has to mingle his or her body and blood with the rest of the world, the people in it, the page; has to find a way to cherish that world even as he or she "struggles to endure it"—Flannery O'Connor's phrase—which is perhaps the best definition of the cross I know.[2]

As a human being, and a Catholic, I saw the cross everywhere. I saw it in actual deserts and I saw it in Koreatown. In the middle of one of the most densely populated sections of Los Angeles, I saw the cross in the desert of my own conflicted heart.

"How can you be Catholic?" people would ask, and I wanted to ask back, but was afraid to, How can you write unless in some sense you have died and been resurrected and, in one way or another, are burning to tell people about it? How can you bear the sorrow of a world in which every last thing passes away without knowing that Christ is right up there on the cross with you?

"How can you be spiritual in L.A.?" someone from back East once asked and, as a car alarm blared, a leaf blower blasted, and I looked over at the children hanging out the windows of the six-story apartment building across the street and screaming, I thought, How can you deal with this ceaselessly pulsing aorta of life with anything *but* spirituality?

Sometimes I would have coffee with my friend Joan, who waitressed at Langer's Deli, or my friend Larry, a janitor at Kaiser. That was what fed me: sitting on the corner of Wilshire and Serrano with traffic streaming by while Joan told me about her troubles with the cook at work, or Larry, who'd done time at every mental health facility from Camarillo to Norwalk before he stopped drinking, reminisced about his "nuthouse romances." What fed me was the miracle of flesh-and-blood, of stories, of the daily struggles that "break, blow, burn" and make us new, as John Donne put it, that give us compassion for the struggles of others.[3]

Inching out into Oxford Avenue on foot, headed to the Pio-Pico library, I would barely be able to make it across, there would be so many cars barreling down from either direction: honking, cutting each other off, jostling for space. It was so easy to feel besieged, so easy to think, *Why are there so many of them?* instead of realizing I'm one of "them" myself; that nobody else likes being crowded either. How can a person live a life of love? I would ask myself as I reached the opposite curb: not love tacked on, added as an afterthought, but shot through every second; flaming out, "like shining from shook foil," as Gerard Manley Hopkins described it in his poem "God's Grandeur."[4]

Wending my way home with my books, my vision temporarily transformed, I would no longer see the refrigerators abandoned on the sidewalk, the triple-parked ice cream trucks, the overflowing trashcans. I'd see flashes of colorful Mexican tile, the 98-cent store mural of waltzing Ajax cans and jitterbugging mops, my favorite flowers: the heliotrope on Ardmore, the wisteria near Harvard, the lemon on Mariposa.

Or maybe it's not that I saw one group of things instead of another but, for one fleeting moment, all simultaneously: the opposites held in balance, a paradigm for the terrible tension and ambiguity of the human condition; the dreadful reality that we can never quite be sure which things we have done and which things we have failed to do; the difference between how we long for the world to be and how it really is a kind of crucifixion in the darkest, most excruciating depths of which we discover—the rear windows of the parked cars I'm walking by now covered with purple jacaranda blossoms—it's not that there's not enough beauty; it's that there's so much it can hardly be borne.

One Monday morning, putting out the garbage as the sky turned pink above the salmon stucco façades, I bent my face to the gardenia in the courtyard, knowing that every shabby corner, every bird and flower and blade of grass, every honking horn and piece of graffiti, every pain and contradiction, deserved a song of praise—"O Sacrament most holy, O Sacrament divine," as we sang at Mass yesterday.

The kids were coming in droves now, making their way to Hobart Middle School—pushing, yelling, throwing their candy wrappers on the sidewalk—and that was a kind of hymn, too. We were all doing our part, their exuberant shouts mingling with the thoughts I would later shape into an essay, all drifting like incense, raised aloft and offered up to the smoggy air above Koreatown. Maybe that's exactly as it should have been. Maybe I needed their noise and they needed my silence. Maybe the song we made together—all of us—was the closest to love we would ever get.

"What are we here for?" Annie Dillard asks in *The Writing Life.* "*Propter chorum,*" the monks say: "for the sake of the choir."[5]

Chapter | Two

HONESTY

....

The School of Beauty

When it comes to hair, I have never acquired the confidence that seems to come so naturally to other fashion-conscious L.A. women. In beauty salons, I feel pale, ill-at-ease, deficient. I am never quite sure what I want and, even if I were, I have never learned the esoteric language that would enable me to communicate it.

"Do you want it layered?" the stylist probes.

"That sounds good," I say, thinking wildly, *What are layers?*

"How short do you want it on top?" they ask.

"I dunno," I mumble. "What do *you* think?"

They tell you to bring in a picture, but the pictures, of course, are always of models or movie stars. I finally figured out it wasn't Meg Ryan's hair I wanted: it was her face, which would look good topped by a yarn wig.

No matter how many hours I spent in beauty salons, no matter how much I paid, my hair never looked the way I wanted it to. I segued from seventy-dollar haircuts to Supercuts to an eight-buck *corte de pelo* in an Hispanic ghetto: My hair looked exactly the same. Why pay a hundred when you can look like hell for ten? I mused.

One day last spring, I went completely over the edge. I decided to get a five-dollar haircut at the Marinello School of Beauty.

First thing Monday morning I showed up at the corner of 3rd and Fairfax, gingerly pushed open the double glass doors, and found myself in a room the size, and with the noise level, of a high school cafeteria. Along beat-up tables, doll heads with luridly made-up faces and hacked-off hair were impaled on spikes, like trophies from a marauding army. Pink plastic curlers littered the floor. A chattering throng of teenagers was rinsing, blow-drying, and teasing a chattering throng of elderly Jewish women.

A short, surly gal with a fake mole on her cheek took my name and a couple of minutes later an intern who looked to be about fourteen came up and smiled, "Hi, I'm Doria." Many of the students seemed to have settled that season on a botanical theme—hair arranged in formal tiers, like terraced gardens set in shellac; crests and swirls evocative of topiary animals—but Doria was a Josephine Baker look-alike, with curlicue eyelashes, hair glued to her skull like a bathing cap and long, graceful limbs.

Doria gave a first-rate wash, training my head with delicious jets of warm water and massaging in a creamy substance that smelled like watermelon. I was just starting to enjoy myself when she twisted a towel around my hair, walked me to an aqua Naugahyde chair, and asked the dreaded question: "How do you want it?"

What I wanted was something arty but uncontrived, cutting-edge but timeless, a style that would telegraph to the world that I am deeply sensitive, daringly iconoclastic and, though far too spiritually evolved to actually care about my personal appearance, attractive in an intriguing, off-kilter sort of way.

"Oh something easy to take care of," I said. "You know, a little off the top."

Doria was the most thorough haircutter I have ever seen. She took a swatch of hair, ran it between her index and middle fingers until maybe a sixty-fourth of an inch was showing, and snipped it off so it was absolutely even. She did this doggedly, conscientiously and unbelievably slowly. I'd figured the less it cost, the less time it would take but I soon realized I'd be lucky if I made it home for dinner.

To pass the time, I began plying Doria with questions, trying to dig up some dirt on the world of beauty schools. It was a two-year program, she informed me; those ratty doll heads cost the students twenty-seven bucks apiece; the teacher's name was Miss Priscilla.

"Is she mean?" I asked hopefully.

"No! Miss Priscilla, she real, real nice."

"Have you ever screwed up someone's hair really bad?" I tried again. "You know, while you were tinting it or something?"

"Nooo," she hooted, "not here—but I was working on my auntie's hair once, trying to bring the color up? And I still don't know what happened, but that hair done turn green. I say, 'Auntie, you don't want to be lookin' in no mirror right now.' Good thing she wasn't working till the next day; had to cut it most all off."

I mulled over this satisfyingly nightmarish scenario for a moment, then turned my attention to the other clients, many of whom were alarmingly illustrative of the long-term effects of bleach, fixatives, and dye. One gal had hair so over-treated it was the texture of fiberglass insulation. Another appeared to be sporting a bright red fright wig, and a third seemed to have clapped a beaver pelt to her scalp. Still, they were having a grand old time, yukking it up with each other, Doria, and the other students with a joyful ease I could only envy.

After an hour, Doria had barely worked her way around from the right side of my head to the back. Ordinarily, this would have made me berserkly impatient, but I loved the way she smelled—a cross between "Evening in Paris" and a Lilt permanent—and her girlish chatter made me feel at home in a way I never had in one of those hoity-toity artiste salons up on Melrose.

Beyond the mirror, palm trees swayed in the parking lot, and the mountains were suspended in a lavender haze. I drowsily closed my eyes. When I opened them, I seemed to have two different hairdos. The top was arranged in a languorous pompadour, the sides were all but shaved and Doria, her elegant hands finally still, was beaming with pride. "Do you like it?" she asked shyly.

It was hideous, of course—I looked like a cross between Roy Orbison and Imogene Coca—but suddenly I saw superimposed on the face of that lovely girl the faces of all the hairdressers who, over the years, had tried their best to make me look good, to guess what I could not articulate, to give me the kind of hair that would make me happy. For one crazy second, my middle-aged face, my gigantic nose, my head full of cowlicks looked almost....

"Doria? " I said firmly. "It's beautiful."

Chapter Three

COURAGE

···
Dorothy Day

On the feast of the Immaculate Conception in 1932, Dorothy Day visited the National Shrine and prayed that, "some way would be opened for me to work for the poor and the oppressed." Right there is the difference between Dorothy Day and me, or maybe you. When I pray, I usually pray for help, for solace, for relief—but I'm not usually thinking of the poor and the oppressed, if you get my drift.

When Dorothy returned from the National Shrine to her apartment in New York, Peter Maurin was waiting on her doorstep, and on May 1, 1933, the Catholic Worker (CW) was born: first a newspaper, then a soup kitchen, then the first "house of hospitality" from which a worldwide lay movement would eventually blossom.

Dorothy's checkered past—the Bohemian nightlife, the flirtation with Communism, the abortion, a common-law marriage—was behind her. In 1927, she'd converted. Then she'd given up Forster Batterham, the resolutely atheistic love of her life, because of his refusal to sanction the baptism of the child they'd conceived together, Tamar. The separation was wrenching—the hardest thing, she later said, that she would ever do.

The Duty of Delight: The Diaries of Dorothy Day spans the years from 1934, a little under a year after the CW began, to nine days before her death in 1980, and nothing could be clearer than that they were written by one fierce, burning flame of a Catholic and a woman. Dorothy herself, notoriously unwilling to suffer fools gladly, said, "Don't call me a saint!" But if the saint is "the person who wills one thing," as Kierkegaard opined, it seemed to me, as I closed this 654-page book, that she came pretty darned close.[1]

"A crowded, confused day with a great desire on my part to write on love and the strange things that happen to you in growing in the love of God," she wrote on September 20, 1953.[2] The love of God was the one thing she willed, and she willed it through poverty, conscripted celibacy, chastity, obedience, labor strikes, jail time, illness, and struggles with the Church; through WWII, the Cold War, and the '60s: "We see her traveling to Cuba on the eve of the Missile Crisis, fasting for peace in Rome during the Second Vatican Council....and standing in solidarity with young men burning their draft cards,"[3] writes editor Robert Ellsberg in his admirable Introduction.

She "willed the one thing" through the Vietnam War; through a showdown with the IRS over her refusal to either pay taxes or register the CW as non-exempt (Dorothy won); through the women's and sexual liberation movements with which, having lived through and witnessed the effects of similar upheavals in the 1920s, she was unable to muster much sympathy. She willed it through moral loneliness. Because when you're Dorothy Day, who is your peer? She had no peer.

Peter Maurin's role was to "enunciate principles"; Dorothy's was to implement them.[4] By May 1935, the circulation of the paper *The Catholic Worker* had already reached an astonishing

100,000. By 1936, the CW had moved into 115 Mott Street in Manhattan, which would remain headquarters for the next fourteen years. The same month they established the first farm outside Easton, Pennsylvania. By 1941, there were already over thirty independent but affiliated CW communities in the United States, Canada, and the United Kingdom.

In 1943, exhausted, Dorothy took a year's leave of absence. She spent several months at a Dominican convent in Farmingdale, Long Island, and used the time typically, not to relax but to spiritually prune herself. ("Exam conscience. It is good to have visitors. One's faults stand out. Also to establish how hard it is to establish regular habits.") Of course, she returned to her beloved Catholic Worker. But for the woman who cofounded, and for decades ran, arguably the most influential Catholic movement of the twentieth century, this habit of examining her conscience persisted throughout her life: "I am oppressed in general by a sense of failure, of sin."[5]

Dorothy frequently quoted the line from Dostoevsky's *The Brothers Karamazov*: "Love in reality is a harsh and dreadful thing compared to love in dreams."[6] The diaries give ample testament to the twin crosses of community and poverty:

> Breakfast a thick slice of dry bread and some very bad coffee.... I have prescribed for myself this day in bed but I keep thinking it is my spirit that is all wrong. I am surrounded by repellent disorder, noise, people, and have no spirit of inner solitude or poverty.[7]

But the real poverty consisted in the conflicts within the community, in meager results, in the fact that no matter how much she accomplished, her efforts never quite sufficed to stem the tide of drunks and crazy people, the shell-shocked, the quarrelsome and argumentative who streamed through the house and whom she made it her life's mission to love and serve.

After the movement she founded had been in existence for forty years, you'd think the folks there would have at least thrown the queen mother/bee a decent party—but no. "May 1. [1973]. Anniversary [of the CW]: Such drunkenness and noise in the house tonight that I could not stand staying downstairs for our 40th birthday anniversary party. A vision of hell. Went upstairs and wept."[8]

Reading Dorothy's diaries, following along with her life month after month, year after year, I'd begun to wonder, *Why is this feeling so familiar?* When I saw the entry about the anniversary party, I realized, *That sounds like my life! That sounds like my family!*

This is the beauty of the diaries. They show us someone just like us, except about ten times more focused, more harder-working, more disciplined. Someone who took note of what she ate that day, of the petty quarrel at dinner, that she rinsed out her underwear at night, but was ten times more able to see God in all of it. The saint isn't the person who refuses to see the meanness and ugliness of the world; the saint is the one humble enough to realize that our humdrum lives, in all their brokenness and glory, are the way we find God.

Because if community was a cross, Dorothy made clear again and again, it was at the same time an enormous blessing. If she was "poor," she reminded herself, she was also rich. As of 1944, she owned only three pairs of stockings ("heavy cotton, grey, tan, and one brown wool"), all of which had come to her "from the cancerous poor, entering a hospital to die.... But the fact remains that I have stockings to cover me when others go cold and naked. The fact remains that I am now listening to a concert—Brahms' 2nd Symphony, joyful music to heal my sadness.... What right have I to recreation? What need have I of recreation?"[9]

Over and over she reminded herself not to judge others, but to love; not to look at the faults in others, but at the faults in herself. She praised St. Thérèse of Lisieux for being as strict with herself as "the Spaniards" (St. John of the Cross and St. Teresa of Avila), but she was equally strict with herself. In all those years, she never allowed herself a word of self-congratulation, never once rested on her laurels. "Physical and spiritual senses need to be 'mortified,' subdued, disciplined,"[10] she observed. That was at the age of seventy-eight.

Who talks about work anymore, that is, hard work as an antidote to our modern illnesses of neurotic guilt and depression? Dorothy did. She cooked, cleaned, planted, resolved disputes, spent hours caring for Tamar (and later, Tamar's nine children). She kept up a voluminous correspondence, hand writing up to ten letters a day (that she didn't keep carbon copies she considered a small act of humility). She was an avid reader: Étienne Gilson, St. Augustine, Jacques Maritain, G.K. Chesterton, Léon Bloy, Charles Péguy, C.S. Lewis, *Butler's Lives of the Saints*; the novelists D.H. Lawrence, Jane Austen, Ignazio Silone. She loved music: Bach, Brahms, opera.

But first and foremost, Dorothy considered herself a writer. "I must learn to contain myself, to do my own work which is writing, correspondence, and the constant study, meditating on both natural and supernatural life."[11] She was continually preoccupied with getting the newspaper to press, writing her column, *On Pilgrimage*, and publishing her books: *The Long Loneliness*, *Loaves and Fishes*, and several others. She was a beautiful, pithy, unsentimental writer, as the diaries alone attest, and those who have tried to write themselves will marvel at her ability to get so much done with such constant inner and outer distractions.

Perhaps the reason she was able to accomplish so much was that she built her life on a bedrock of daily devotions: the Divine Office, rosaries, vigils, prayer, fasts, and always, the Mass. For over forty years, Dorothy went to Mass almost every day. In fact, perhaps her greatest accomplishment was her blending of the active and the contemplative lives in a way that was entirely traditional and yet entirely modern and new. For all her radicalism, she was as observant as any medieval nun. For all her activity, she was at heart a mystic:

> I was overwhelmed at being right over the altar, the Blessed Sacrament out of my sight but so near, and the strong sound of Gregorian rising in waves of adoration and praise, which seemed to fling themselves joyfully against the altar.[12]

Day wrote, "I am not interested in politics or elections."[12] She was interested in the homeless, the hungry, the forsaken. She was interested in peace and justice and brotherly love, and she believed that all genuine love is grounded in Christ-like self-sacrifice.

Throughout her life, she lectured, attended conferences, and traveled around the country by bus to visit the burgeoning number of sister houses. In July 1973, she accepted an invitation to speak at Joan Baez's Institute for the Study of Nonviolence in Palo Alto, and used the occasion also to picket with the United Farm Workers (UFW) in Delano. It would be her final arrest. "The true anarchist asks nothing for himself, he is self-disciplined, self-denying, accepting the Cross, without asking sympathy, without complaint."[14] Her words could have been a caption for the famous photo of that day in Delano: mouth set, eyes fierce, staring down an armed policeman.

She continued her travels in California, including a visit to Los Angeles. When I read the entry for August 19, 1973, my heart leapt: "Sister Catherine [Morris] (Holy Child) is here at A.H. [Ammon Hennacy] house 5 days weekly. Fasting."[15] I knew Catherine Morris from visits to the L.A. Catholic Worker community at Hennacy House! To know she has devoted her life to following in Day's footsteps was a thrill indeed.

One other entry stayed with me, the entry for August 24, 1973, five days later: "Mass at St. Basil's, to confession to Cardinal McIntyre. Many at Mass, great and beautiful church often crowded."[16]

St. Basil's was in K'town, and the morning after I finished reading the diaries I walked to Mass there myself. Dorothy was much on my mind and when a homeless woman—no shoes, no teeth—noisily stretched out in the pew behind me, I realized at once the encounter was no accident. She was one of "the least of these" and as she moaned and muttered and the entire congregation edged gingerly back, I realized in a whole new way that if you're going to live out the Gospels you can't have a life that's separate. You can't have too much to lose in the way of time, money, belongings. You have to at least be willing to share these things.

So when Mass was over, I turned and made a point of meeting the woman's eyes. Smiling back, she asked, "Do you have a dollar?" If I'd been Dorothy Day, I could have said, "Do you need a place to stay? Come home with me." But I'm not, so I did the next best thing. I said, "Yeah, I have a dollar, but do you want me to take you downtown, too? Cause I know where there's a soup kitchen if you're hungry and the people there will know of some shelters."

"No thanks, hon," she said, "I just want a dollar."

"Are you sure?" I said. "My car's back at my apartment but I'd be glad to go get it and drive you down there"

"I just want a dollar," she replied, and in the nicest possible way added, "Actually, do you have five dollars? I need to get back to Compton."

Sure you do, I thought, and gave her five, which seemed to delight us both.

In the annals of human interchange it wasn't much, but if not for Dorothy Day, I might not have even considered giving up part of my precious morning. If not for Dorothy Day and the good, good people at the L.A. Catholic Worker, who have been comforting the afflicted and afflicting the comfortable since 1970, I might not have known where to offer to take her. If I hadn't spotted a copy of *The Long Loneliness* by accident fifteen years ago, I might never have converted at all. I might never have stumbled upon the folks at Hennacy House, who in their quiet way, and perhaps unbeknownst to them, have been a comfort, a support, a lodestar, and a challenge to continually examine my beliefs and grow.

Apropos of daily Mass, Dorothy had written, "He took upon himself our humanity that we might share in his divinity. We are nourished by his flesh that we may grow to be other Christs. I believe this literally, just as I believe the child is nourished by the milk from his mother's breast."[17]

I believe that, too.

What honor, respect, devotion, and love we owe this remarkable woman who, like us, doubted, sweated, bled, believed, and—as we can only pray we will—stayed the course. It takes a saint, or at least a Dorothy Day, to live a life that to its smallest moment shows that solace comes from helping the other person. It takes a Dorothy Day to remind us that learning to love our neighbor requires a kind of continuing, ongoing crucifixion. If not for Christ, where would any of us go, Lord? So under his gaze, we put our arms around each other, the homeless woman and I, and walked out of St. Basil's together.

Chapter | Four

GRATITUDE
Blue Skies

I grew up in New Hampshire, and in all my most vivid child-hood memories, I am shivering. For the better part of the year, I waited for the school bus in weather so cold my teeth ached, stood hunched against frigid winds at recess and came home to a mother who considered it perfectly normal for citizens of the twentieth century to inhabit a house the temperature of an igloo.

At night, I climbed between sheets that felt as if they'd been stored in a refrigerator and, in the morning, woke to a room whose air had the raw bite of the tundra. One fairy tale char-acter in particular had a devastating hold on my psyche: Hans Christian Andersen's Little Match Girl, the gentle street urchin who froze to death on New Year's Eve.

Those long, bleak winters, interspersed with the achingly ephemeral days of summer, shaped a worldview that I have spent most of my adult life trying to change. They made me believe in a God who made you earn every happy moment by imposing a hundred moments of misery, who snatched things away just as your fingers closed around them, who had a block of ice in the socket reserved for a warm, beating heart.

They are a big part of the reason why, in 1990, I moved to place where, by Eastern standards, it is summer all the time. My then-husband and I were lonely and broke and afraid we had made a mistake in moving so far away from everything we knew. But on the south side of the nondescript stucco house we'd rented, a camellia bloomed that first uncertain March, tipsy with flowers so pink and lush they made me want to throw a party. Such wanton extravagance—in March!—while in New England, spring was heralded by a single demure crocus pushing from a crust of snow.

Besides the camellia, the yard was bare; the previous tenants had used the lawn, which was as hard and dry as concrete, for a driveway. That anything could take root there seemed impossible but, inspired by the succession of balmy days, I turned on the rusted sprinkler every night. After a few weeks, a soft shroud of green appeared, which eventually needed mowing. We sent away for seeds and bulbs, dug up flowerbeds, planted Jerusalem sage, evening primrose, coral bells. We started a compost heap and put in a patch of collards and sugar snap peas, a bumper crop whose tendrils rose eight feet high. On weekends, in the midst of this bounty, we dragged our lawn chairs out front and read in the sun. My husband sometimes wore his carpenter's overalls and dispensed farming advice to curious passersby. We met everyone on our block that way.

We moved out of that house after two years: Driving by a few months later, I saw the lawn was once again as hard and dry as concrete. And though our lives as well were eventually marked by many changes—the aging and deaths of our parents, major surgery, divorce—I am still overwhelmed with gratitude that I no longer live in a place where summer seems to be a fleeting interlude of happiness for which winter is the grim, inexorable price.

I have even become grateful for the frigid winters I endured for thirty-eight years, because the memory of them makes California weather seem continually miraculous in a way I am not sure is possible for those who were born and bred here. I have never learned to refrain from exclaiming, "Isn't it gorgeous out!" to natives who meet my enthusiasm with bored, blank stares. I have never quite lost the feeling of having stumbled, undeserving, upon an ever-replenishing piece of luck. There is something in this of the immigrant's dream fulfilled, and part of me still lives with the immigrant's lingering fear that one morning there will be a knock on the door and they'll make me go back home.

On any given day in, say, November or January or March, when people back East are getting snow down their necks and scraping ice from their windshields; when here, sunlight the color of honey streams down the golden canyons like a benediction, I sometimes think that, in Los Angeles, the story of the Little Match Girl has been rewritten. This time her father doesn't beat her; she doesn't freeze to death; they don't find her thinly clad body, blue with cold, on New Year's Day.

This time the visions of the gleaming stove, the fragrant goose, the Christmas tree with its candles like stars streaking across the sky do not fade in the time it takes a match to burn down. Instead, they are resurrected, day after perfect day, as our simplest, most essential blessings: Light. Food. Warmth.

Chapter Five

CHASTITY

Save All of Yourself for the Wedding

I don't think purity is mere innocence; I don't think babies and idiots possess it. I take it to be something that comes either with experience or with Grace so that it can never be naïve.[1]

—FLANNERY O'CONNOR

One recent night I went to dinner at the house of a gay friend I'll call Dave. The other two guests, Todd and Pete, were also gay. Somehow we got to talking about childhood trauma. All three told of being molested before the age of ten: one by a female babysitter, one by an older boy, one by his father. All three spoke of how, as adults, they instantly fled if left alone in a room with a person under the age of eighteen of either sex for fear of being accused of pedophilia.

One said his earliest memories, when he was trying to clamber to his feet to take his first steps, were of his mother shrieking, *"Don't walk like a girl!!"* He had helplessly raised his hands, as if to defend himself; the limp-wristed gay stereotype, we observed, may emblemize an unconscious reversion to the fetal position.

All my friends at dinner that night had been sexualized before puberty. All struggled with low self-esteem, painful relationships, and addictions of various kinds. All had been working for years toward inner healing, and were trying to use their gifts in service to the world.

My heart bled for them, and for all victims of incest, abuse, and sexual violence. We went on to speak of how pornography is endemic in both the gay and straight worlds, and of a TED talk Pete had seen on the way porn dulls the capacity both for pleasure and for joy. He mentioned that researchers today have trouble conducting studies because they can't find control groups: they can hardly find a single adult male who has never seen porn in one form or another. A whole generation is coming up that has been raised on porn, whose psyches, nervous systems, brains, and bodies are being formed by porn. The average age at which boys start watching porn now is eleven.[2]

As I listened to my friends, I suddenly thought about the gift, the mystery, of simply sitting there with them silently, invisibly chaste. I had never been so keenly aware of my body as a temple of the Holy Spirit (I can never use that phrase without thinking of the masterful Flannery O'Connor short story of the same name and snickering). I had never felt so deeply the value of—I'm just going to use the word, however incongruous it may sound in connection with myself—purity.

"Purity strikes me as the most mysterious of the virtues," O'Connor wrote, "and the more I think about it the less I know about it."[3] It may also be the most difficult of the virtues to speak of. Like humility, to even speak of your own is to sully it. And because we laugh at it, and ridicule it, and fetishize it with "chastity talks" (please!), we have yet to plumb its depths.

As O'Connor said, purity is not innocence: For years I was a barfly: the lower-down and dirtier the bar, the better. I've slept with married men. I've had three abortions. So purity is not innocence, but neither is purity some creepy, snow-maiden, don't-touch-me weirdness. Purity has juice at the center of it or it's not purity; it's repression, it's fear, it's withholding, it's fossilizing one's "virginity" in amber. It's playing hard-to-get that's veered off to pathology.

The erotic urge behind purity is more, not less, intense than the erotic urge behind sex alone. Authentic purity is fueled by procreative, erotic energy that's been brought to a white-hot flame—and channeled.

I came into the Church in 1996. I've tried to remain faithful to her teachings, on sex and everything else. When I haven't, I've availed myself of the sacrament of reconciliation (among other things) and sincerely tried to do better.

I've stumbled, I've failed, but one thing my efforts toward fidelity have given me is some rough purity of heart. I go to confession because I believe that what we do and think matters. I go because I believe someone, somewhere, needs me to be pure. Maybe it's the father of a ten-year-old girl who is contemplating molesting her. Maybe it's an adult who was abused by a priest as a kid and is about to abuse his own kid. Maybe it's the teenagers who are about to lynch Matthew Shepard.

That night at dinner, I looked around at the faces of my friends—good men, creative men, kind men, who had suffered deeply—and I thought of the times I'd trudged to confession, usually on Saturday afternoons, alone. I remembered waiting alone one winter afternoon in a church in Arroyo Seco, New Mexico, for the priest to arrive, and looking out the window at the bare trees, and thinking that we don't know the mercy of God. We make rules, as we must—because to have a free-for-all makes for a way worse bondage than rules—but at the end of the day we will be judged on love. For all the ways we've fallen short, aimed for pleasure divorced from joy, thought of ourselves instead of the whole world, we'll be judged on one thing: how we treated the least of these.

We'll be judged on whether we've woken up to the fact that the whole joy of life is admitting our brokenness, falling to our knees in gratitude, moving our chair a little to make room so that the person beside us can sit at the table, too. We've already been forgiven; are forgiven even as we're falling short. I wonder if we go to confession mostly so that we can forgive ourselves.

To strive for purity in this culture, even privately, is to feel oneself a laughingstock, grotesquely out of step, a freak. But sitting quietly amidst my friends, I "saw" in a way I never had before that my life in Christ had borne fruit. My prayers, my tears, my sorrow, my longing for wholeness, for all of us, had been in a sense for them. Christ had made use of the long, slow discipline that I'd been tempted to think had gone for naught. All along I had been offering up the only, the deepest, the first and last thing I had: my body.

Catholic novelist François Mauriac observed, "We do not know the worth of one single drop of blood, one single tear."[4] We don't know the worth of a single tear, and we don't know the worth of entering into a kind of voluntary exile out of love. We don't know the worth of the simple bodily presence of someone who lives by a creed that costs.

But while purity isn't innocence, neither is it penance. To, say, try to atone for my abortions by taking a vow of celibacy: no. Too harsh, too much self-will, too much focus on *my* sacrifice. No priest has ever suggested such thing, or anything close to it. The question is never, "How huge a sacrifice can I make?" but rather, "How can I best contribute to the world?"

Purity is the conviction that we are all pearls of great price: not to be violated, tampered with, used loosely, or given away for less than we are worth or to someone who's incapable of understanding our value. Christianity is all invitation and all gift. To offer up my body also gives me a way not to die of the sorrow of the world; not to be crushed by my inadequacy, my seeming meagerness, my inability to "help."

So this chastity—in my case actually celibacy, which, believe me, has not been entirely voluntary, nor always joyfully, wholeheartedly embraced—is a great mystery. I have often felt like a loser, an aging outcast, an exile. I have worried that I am incapable of giving and receiving love. I have of course wondered whether I've embraced the teachings of the Church or whether I've parlayed my fear of intimacy and my wounds into some kind of crackpot "holiness."

Pop psychology encourages me to view my situation as "sexual anorexia" but I know that's wrong because I am more, not less, available to the world—and I am also less lonely. I'm alone a lot of the time, but I'm not plagued by loneliness, scourged by loneliness, as I have been for much of my life. I feel useful, needed, at my full powers as a writer and a human being, part of an adventure infinitely greater than myself.

My friends know I'm Catholic. They know I'm single. They know I care for them and for their spiritual well-being, and I know they care for mine. Beyond that, we don't go. They don't know the years of sorrow, of working through my neuroses and blocks, of loneliness unto death, of searching, of finding. They know nothing of my life in Christ and little of my sexual and emotional struggles.

I can hardly speak of them myself. I remember lying on my bed one afternoon many years ago, in anguish over a man I loved and who did not love me, or not in the way I wanted him to. I thought "I am either going to drink again or I am going to kill myself." And I wouldn't do either of those things. Drinking would be tantamount to suicide, and I would not choose death. Someone would have to kill me first; and at the time, I wished someone *would* kill me. My God, Lord, how long? I thought. How much longer? Will this suffering that I had already endured for years never end? And I had a very short but very decisive moment of clarity. I thought, Christ never lied. He never said that following him was going to be easy. He said, "For the gate is narrow and the road is hard that leads to life, and there are few who find it," (Matthew 7:14), and that's because to go through the narrow gate hurts. It hurts like hell. It hurt like hell for him. And he never lied.

So in the deepest part of my being I made a decision, and the decision was simply to trust, like Job, who said, "See, [God] will kill me; I have no hope; but I will defend my ways to his face" (Job 13:15). It wasn't so much that I had to give all hope of every having a partner, of having sex, of being married, of bearing fruit with a man; it was a matter of giving up my whole self, my capacity for romantic and sexual love included, for God to do with as he would.

I'd tried going after what and who *I* wanted. I'd tried all my life. I'd never come to the deepest fulfillment and I also had never given my *all,* which I think is truly the deepest desire of the human heart. We want to give ourselves fully, to forget ourselves, of which orgasm is a foretaste, an emblem, an echo—and of course, why it's so compelling.

I'm human. I'll never be entirely free, nor entirely well. I'll never know my truest, deepest motives, which at best, remain mixed. But if I waited for my motives to be pure, I'd never take any stand at all. Lost sheep that I am, I have cast my lot with Christ, who said, "My sheep know my voice." Not *that* kind of voice, not for me, anyway; not visions, not *deus ex machina* miracles. Rather the silent conviction, to the depth of my being, that we are connected: cell to cell, bone to bone, flesh to flesh, body to body, spirit to spirit, tiny flickering light to light. You don't come to that conviction through philosophy or theology. Those things may lead you to the threshold but at some point you have to trust, even though "God will kill me." And he does kill us.

God kills us, and then he brings us to life again: the same, but different. St. Maria Goretti consented to be stabbed to death at the age of eleven rather than yield her virginity, not because she was some shrinking-violet Victorian who became faint at the thought of sex, but because she knew her full worth. She had taken the full measure of herself, her mind, her strength, her soul, her heart.

When you take the full measure of yourself, in Christ, you, too, know your infinite value to the rest of the world, even if the world never knows or sees one thing about you. Every hair on your head is numbered. You are worth more than many sparrows because you have lusts and longings and desires unto death and out of love, you consent hold the tension of the conflict. And your infinite value doesn't cease when you die. It lives on, into eternity.

Everyone can make the prayer of the body. "It is possible for everyone, always, if they have a body," wrote Caryll Houselander in *The Mother of Christ*.[5] "It means offering our bodies as a sacrifice for mankind. It needs no sweet meditation, no eloquence of words, no sensible fervor. It can be made in aridity, weariness, dullness, boredom, pain, in temptation, in any circumstances at all, by anyone."

To the world this is folly. That is because even we believers shrink from the radical call of Christianity, which is not only to give our whole selves but to be ridiculed for it, misunderstood for it; to be charged with a *lack* of compassion. I thought of all the people who would jeer, "Who cares that you haven't had sex in ten years; why don't you picket for gay marriage?" I thought, again, of Flannery O'Connor, who observed, "The Catholic novelist believes that you destroy your freedom by sin; the modern reader believes, I think, that you gain it in that way. There is not much possibility of understanding between the two."[6]

In *The Lord*, Romano Guardini observed:

> Every Christian one day reaches the point where he too must be ready to accompany the Master into destruction and oblivion: into that which the world considers folly, that which for his own understanding is incomprehensible, for his own feeling intolerable. Whatever it is to be: suffering, dishonor, the loss of loved ones, or the shattering of a lifetime oeuvre, this is the decisive test of his Christianity. Will he shrink back before the ultimate depths, or will he be able to go all the way and thus win his share of the life of Christ? What is it we fear in Christianity if not precisely this demand? That is why we try to water it down to a less disturbing system of "ethics" or "Weltanschauung" or what have you. But to

be a Christian means to participate in the life of Christ—
all of it; only the whole brings peace.[7]

That is what we call each other to as Catholics: the highest level
of awakening, the highest level of sacrifice, the highest level of
participation, the highest level of love.

So, we give all that we have. We are like the widow's last two
mites, and like mites, we are unseen, tossed aside, hidden, of no
account in the ledger of the world. We give all we have anyway, in
silence, scorned as bigots, ridiculed as nutcases, our hearts aflame
with the hope that one day, perhaps not in our lifetimes, another
human heart may catch flame as well.

I didn't tell my friends any of this that night. I didn't inform
them that gay sex is wrong. I didn't mentally check to assure that
my thoughts were in accord with the finer points of John Paul II's
Theology of the Body. I said, "That must be hard, thinking people
are going to accuse you of pedophilia." I spoke a bit of my own
lifelong sense of exile, of how relationships to me have always
meant more or less unalloyed pain.

We went on to speak of movies and books. We ate panna cotta
with praline and raspberries. I left the three of them, still drinking
coffee, and walked home alone, beneath the moon.

"Save all of yourself for the wedding though / nobody knows
when or if it will come," wrote Brazilian poet Carlos Drummond
de Andrade.[8]

We offer up all that we are as we wait, in secret hope, for the
wedding. And receive it back—a hundredfold, a thousandfold, as
I did that night from my friends—as a gift.

Chapter Six

GENEROSITY

At the Central Library

Some years ago, I spent the winter hanging around downtown L.A., trudging the filthy, noisy streets with my used laptop on my back: gray sky, honking horns, sunless streets hemmed in by grimy buildings.

Christ had nowhere to lay his head and neither, it felt like, did I. I was roaming around downtown because Monday through Thursday my then-husband was at home during the day in our one-bedroom apartment, and I'd taken to coming to the Central Library to write.

One morning as I was walking down 5th to Olive, a toothless woman in white go-go boots tottered over with her palm upraised. With a sigh, I took out my wallet. "Oh, look, she gave all she had," the woman crooned, as I peeled off a dollar from a wad of tens and fives. I wondered if she was mocking me, remembering Luke's parable of the widow who gave her last coin. I looked at her again, hard. "All she had," she murmured lovingly, smiling her toothless, inscrutable smile.

This is getting creepy, I thought. *Biblical scenes coming to life on the streets of twenty-first-century L.A.?* I looked around: a Nautilus Plus, a Jack 'n' the Box, a mazelike, quintessentially Southern California parking structures. How had it come to pass that I was consorting with the modern-day equivalent of lepers and mutes? If something didn't break with my career pretty soon, next thing I knew I'd be standing on a street corner croaking to random passersby, "Pick up your mat and walk!" and, "By his stripes, you were healed!"

The library featured a whole community of folks who considered the place their daytime home. An elderly man with a ripped sports coat, K-Swiss sneakers—as if in his spare time he played tennis—and a tic that compelled him to continually brush an imaginary cobweb from his face. A fat guy with thick black glasses, mad scientist hair, and pockets stuffed with papers, snoozing in an armchair. A guard in a satin bomber jacket patrolled the stacks telling people they weren't allowed to sleep in the carrels, or shushing some lost soul who was talking to himself, or warning me to take my laptop with me when I went to the bathroom because otherwise someone might steal it.

With my orange earplugs jammed in to block out the noise, I kept remembering an essay I'd read by Richard Rohr in which he described going to a monastery and meeting one particular monk, a hermit who lived in a hut in the mountains. He'd met the guy once, they'd chatted briefly and then, twenty years later, he returned to this same monastery. By chance, Rohr ran into the same monk while walking in the woods. Thinking there was no way the hermit would recognize him after all that time, and not wanting to disturb the man's solitude, Rohr was prepared to pass silently by. Instead, the hermit stopped, embraced him, and began talking as if they'd broken off a discussion not five minutes before. "Richard!" he said. "You get to preach and I don't. When you're out there preaching, please tell the people one thing. *God is not "out there."*"[1]

After I'd finished the day's writing, I often trolled for books: religion on lower level 3, art on the second floor, literature on the third. One book that made a deep impression on me that winter was Margaret Wertheim's *The Pearly Gates of Cyberspace: A History of Space from Dante to the Internet*. It described the fascinating world of quantum physics and space-time theories in terms even a science ignoramus like me could understand. One incident I found particularly gripping was the 1920 discovery, by a Russian named Theodor Kaluza, of a fifth dimension. I'd always thought of a dimension as being unbelievably big but, according to this theory, just the opposite was true. Wertheim wrote:

> It was no wonder we had not observed the extra dimension, because it is absolutely minute. Its circumference was just 10 to the minus 23rd power centimeters—a hundred billion billion times smaller than the nucleus of an atom! So small was Kaluza's dimension that even if we ourselves were the size of atoms we would *still* not notice it. Yet this tiny dimension could be responsible for all electromagnetic radiation....[2]

What could be more exciting, I thought. It was a paradigm for the smallness, the poverty, the hiddenness of Christ! And not an inert hiddenness, but a dynamic hiddenness: every infinitesimal thought, word, act simultaneously occurring on five, eight, now, they were coming to believe, eleven dimensions. Nothing wasted, everything connected: the woman in the white go-go boots, the man in the K-Swiss sneakers, me laboring over my laptop—not out there, but in here. Of course biblical scenes were taking place on the streets of twenty-first-century L.A.; they'd been taking place every second, in every human encounter, for thousands of years.

One drizzly morning not long after I'd finished Wertheim's book, I was walking past the reflecting pool in the library courtyard, headed inside as usual. I'd packed some hummus, an orange, and a container of white beans with kale for my noontime break. Not far from the steps was a ripped sleeping bag with a person-shaped lump inside. "Poor soul," I thought and—partly to score possible spiritual brownie points, partly out of a genuine, if uncharacteristic, surge of generosity—decided to give the person my lunch.

"I'm going to leave some food out here," I reported in a soothing voice. I'd pictured a wraithlike being beneath the blanket: half-dead, far too exhausted to rouse him- or herself from slumber and acknowledge me. Instead, the figure sat bolt upright, as if a spring had been released, and a hand pulled back a stocking cap to reveal the face of a handsome, strapping fellow in his early thirties. "Why thank you, ma'am, that's very kind of you," he said cheerfully, peering into the bag. "I'll eat this right away!"

I was starving by noon, but somehow I knew we were both going to make it.

Chapter | Seven

WISDOM

Send My Roots Rain

Let me say it again: whether we experience it as painful
or pleasurable, *the night is dark for our protection.* We
cannot liberate ourselves; our defenses and resistances
will not permit it, and we can hurt ourselves in the
attempt. To guide us toward the love that we most desire,
we must be *taken* where we could not and would not
want to go on our own. And lest we sabotage the journey,
we must not know where we are going. Deep in the darkness, way beneath our senses, God is instilling "another;
better love" and "deeper, more urgent longings" that
empower our willingness for all the necessary relinquish-
ments along the way.[1]

—GERALD MAY, *The Dark Night of the Soul*

In the fall of 2007 I set out in my '96 Celica for a cross-country
pilgrimage. I was in the throes of what I thought at the time was
an incomprehensibly demoralizing unrequited love and what
I now know was more like an epic codependent enmeshment.
Whatever it was, I'd tried everything: moral inventories, the sacrament of confession, twelve-step groups. *Am I supposed to be a
nun?* I wondered. *Is there something so fundamentally unhinged,
so narcissistically wounded, so egregiously selfish about me that
I am unable (after a sixteen-year marriage) to have a "normal"
relationship?*

And so I took off, from the extreme southwest of the country to the extreme northeast: namely, from L.A., where I lived, to the coast of New Hampshire, where I'd been raised. In a kind of desperate, atavistic, run-out-of-ideas pilgrim urge, I'd decided to make a ritual trip home to my mother, who at the time had early-stage Alzheimer's, knowing that once we moved her to assisted living, which was imminent, there would likely be no home, ever again, to go to.

I left on Friday, August 17, and I returned on Thursday, October 4. I didn't drive the byways. I drove the interstates, as fast and long and hard as I could: five hundred, sometimes six hundred miles at a stretch. I stayed at the cheapest chain hotels I could find. I ate crackers, sardines, and dried fruit. I went to Mass every day. That was how I ordered my trip. That was what made my trip a kind of very ordinary, but very definite pilgrimage. I didn't know anything else but to stay as close to Jesus as I possibly could. I visited family, friends, the Franciscan Appalachian Hermitage, and Graceland. And every morning I went to MassTimes.org and figured out where I needed to drive to so I could find a church that had Mass the next day which—that's another story, but believe me—was not all that easy.

Over the course of a month and a half, I made it to New Hampshire, wended my way back toward California, and washed up on the shores of the Benet Hill (all women's) Monastery in Colorado Springs, where I more or less collapsed and stayed for a week. I felt nothing. I knew nothing. I was not in despair but I had been stripped down as far as, at the time, I could go.

This is an account of the last two days before I returned to L.A.

Tuesday, October 2nd.

The Memorial of the Guardian Angels.

Mass at Holy Trinity Church in Colorado Springs.

"Ye Watchers and Ye Holy Ones," we sang in closing, and when I approached my fully packed car afterward—for I'd checked out of the monastery—I realized the pilgrimage was over. Just like that, the pilgrimage was over. I didn't have to be on pilgrimage anymore; didn't have to find a church for the next day. With the angels guarding me, I could begin to mull over this trip that I'd undertaken in blindness; convinced, however, that whatever unfolded during its course was a necessary part of my spiritual awakening that could not have happened any other way.

First, I put my head on the steering wheel and cried: tears of joy? gratitude? sorrow? I didn't know. And then I was headed home, on Route 50W through Colorado, through gorgeous mountains for miles and miles beside canyons, and for a long time along a rushing green river lined with bushy gold-yellow flowers, like stands of lush goldenrod, and on to the top of Monarch Mountain, which was covered in snow, and the aspens all yellow, listening to Arvo Pärt's *Berlin Mass* three times straight through, because I hadn't heard any music for days and Pärt was all I felt like listening to.

Getting out to stretch my legs around noon, I saw that my Blundstone boots—ankle-length, pull-on boots from Australia I'd had for years—were beginning to fall apart, with little chunks of sole peeling off. They'd carried me far; they looked like the workers' boots in that Van Gogh painting. Maybe I'd retire them when I returned to a little glass reliquary, suitable for viewing.

Finally I got on Interstate 70 and saw a sign, "Las Vegas, 512 miles," so I thought, *OK, I'm gonna go halfway to Vegas.* Pretty soon, though, when I was almost in Utah, I saw another sign, "I-15, 240 miles," so I thought, *OK, then, I'll do that; I'll drive as far as the 15 and call it a day.* Utah is great. You cross the border and the sign says "Visitor Information, 40 miles": like, why rush? "No Services 60 miles," the next sign reads; then there's a lone exit with a single gas station followed by another sign: "No Services 110 miles."

Also, the route signs have a little beehive on them, and another nice thing is the state of Utah maintains "view points." I pulled over at one, which featured a trail to a precipice that no one in his or her right mind would have gone within a quarter of a mile of, so I stood respectfully by my car and "viewed" the seemingly miles-deep canyon from there.

Back on the road, the trees were breathtaking. Butternut, 24-carat gold trees, piercing yellow. Orange, like celestial honey. *Oh my God. Thank you, Lord.*

Junction I-15, 92 miles. Okay, baby, I'd be within shouting distance—that is, a long day's drive, from L.A.—by 6:00 p.m. When I did reach the 15, I was so stoked that I decided to keep going. My plan for my last night had been to camp out, as I had done on my first night, way back in August, at Saguaro National Park outside Tucson.

My ex-husband, Tim, and I had stayed a couple of times at a cabin in Kanarraville, Utah, outside Zion, so I pulled off from the I-15 there and drove through town, hoping at least to find a mom-and-pop hotel, but it was off season. The absence of people made the town feel kind of eerie, and me feel sad, though I'd felt that way even when I'd been there with Tim: I was just a little lonely, and wanted to experience, even if only for a few minutes, a place I'd been with another human being who had more or less loved me.

But nothing was going on in Kanarraville so I continued on, looking for a place off the 15 where we'd once found a campground, and where I had made a mental note to stay another time. I tried the Toquerville exit, where a marker at the ramp said "Day's Inn .9," or so I thought, but perhaps the sign had read "9" or even "19," as I drove many miles and saw no Days Inn nor any other hotel. So I turned around and went back to the freeway.

Next I took the Leeds exit because a sign said "Silver Reef" and I thought Silver Reef might have been the campground I'd been thinking of. But the road was pitch black, and I stumbled my way (yes, you can stumble in a car) up a hill only to find a rash of housing developments. So I wound back down and on to the Leeds Hotel and RV Park, which was full of RVs but dead quiet, and when I rang the bell at the office nobody answered.

No room at the inn, I thought, kept going, and next tried the Washington exit. I drove past one of those giant, scary-looking chain hotels—La Quinta maybe—and then I was on some kind of rushing, rushing turnpike or boulevard, and the night was so dark and the cars were coming at me from behind so fast that I felt frightened—I'm used to L.A. where everything is fluorescent bright at all hours—and sat in a left turn lane for what seemed like ten minutes waiting for the green arrow, made a U-turn, and fled yet again to the freeway.

I'd given up on the idea of camping out for the night, and so pressed on to the good-sized town of St. George (site of the trial of fundamentalist Mormon/serial polygamist/husband to seventy women Warren Jeffs), saw a Motel 6 sign, took that exit, and was checked in by a sullen teenage girl with glasses and zits. When I got up to Room 251, the cheap greenish-blue wall-to-wall carpet, I swear, was wet. I mean beyond damp—wet. Totally gross. So in a way, I *was* camping.

I walked out onto the balcony to check out my neighbors; then, exhausted, I brushed my teeth and crawled into bed feeling quite sorry for myself. Taking up two rooms below, I'd seen, were a group of Armenians: an older chain-smoking guy walking the pug, a baby crying, the rest of the extended family shouting back and forth like the whole place was their living room. In the next room over a fat woman and her fat ten-year-old son apparently could not figure out the ultra-complicated task of opening and shutting their door as every time I was on the verge of falling asleep I was jarred awake by the sound of its heavy, annoying click/thud. The sullen gal at the front desk was at this very moment no doubt checking in hordes more of the nomad hoi polloi. How had I ended up in this hell-hole, especially the last night of my trip that I'd so wanted to be special? Middle America was so repulsive! Look what we'd done!—with our Denny's and our Wendy's and our *gruesomely damp carpets*.

One more night, I was sleeping alone, and I remembered spiritual writer Ron Rolheiser saying that to sleep alone is a kind of poverty, as keenly felt and difficult to endure as any poverty. Christ's voluntary celibacy, Rolheiser held, was not meant to imply that celibacy is a higher calling than marriage. Instead, Christ had wanted to be in solidarity with all the people in the world who sleep alone involuntarily—the unattractive, the aged, the emotionally or physically wounded, the unlucky.[2]

So I thought of Christ; I tried to be with Christ. And after a while I realized that if Christ were around today, these were just the kinds of places he'd be hanging around at. He'd be at the Taco Bells and the Wendy's; he'd be at the Super 8s and the Motel 6s with the plastic ice buckets, the molded acrylic chairs with cushions the color of dried blood, the rooms overlooking the telephone poles and the freeway, the swimming pool in the middle of the parking lot.

He'd be with all the people I'd just come in contact with: the pimply check-in gal whose boyfriend had probably just dumped her, the Armenian guy who was walking his dog, the fat lady and her fat son. He'd be with the families who'd scrimped all year; with the couple I'd seen earlier laboriously lugging a Rubbermaid bin of food from their pickup, securing the truck bed with a bright blue tarp, leaning against the hood, eating dinner from red plastic bowls as they watched the sun set. He'd be with the people who were headed in from, and back out to, the mountains, the deserts, the view points, their hearts hemorrhaging, their souls hungry for meaning.

He'd be with me.

I didn't want to be as unremarkable, as lost and misguided, with as seemingly little hope or promise as everyone else. But I was. And it was all right. I was almost home. Home, from which I'd come so far, and where I still had so far to go. Home, a whole City of Guardian Angels. Home, the land Joan Didion had memorialized in "Some Dreamers of the Golden Dream."

Watching the pink fade from the eastern sky the next morning, I thought *I'm within seven or eight hours of home now.* I'd had to be alone for a while, but now I was called to rejoin the human race. I had friends to see and more work to do—with the help of people I trusted, for I couldn't do the work alone. More learning compassion for others, but also for myself; more discerning how to give all of myself to God; more examination of conscience, uncovering of character defects, and praying that they be removed.

As Walker Percy said, referring to Catholicism: "What else is there?"[3] Because you can subscribe to Jungian thought with its archetypes, symbols, and dreams: all utterly valid and part of the light; you can detach from your thoughts through meditation: part of the light; you can experience the healing power of nature: part of the light; you can see and rightfully rail against the ways that we sometimes appropriate "religion" and ideas and belief systems to our own ends, and worse, try to impose them on others: part of the light; you can unearth the ways your childhood has shaped and wounded you: part of the light.

But you will never get to the truth and become your most authentic self without seeing your own incredible propensity for darkness and sin; without acknowledging the ways that you have hurt, or are capable of hurting, others. "The operation of the church is entirely set up for the sinner;" wrote Flannery O'Connor, "which creates much misunderstanding among the smug."[4]

When one of us is found—however provisionally—we're all found. When any one of us comes home—though, inevitably, we'll leave again someday—we all come home. Home: grit from L.A.'s blessedly polluted air veiling the hardwood floors. Home: the tinny music of the ice cream truck floating through French windows. My apartment would need dusting and polishing, and the dusting would radiate out to everybody. The plants on my balcony—the agaves and cacti and succulents that brought me so much joy!—would need watering, and the watering would reverberate out to the whole cosmos. I would get back to my desk, and the writing would forge a new connection to the rest of the world. (From the notebooks of Camus: Maman. "What was her silence saying. What was this mute and smiling mouth screaming. We will be resurrected.")[5]

Outside my window at the Motel 6 lay the swimming pool, and beyond, descending in order of height, loomed a yellow and red six-sided Denny's sign; a red, white, and blue Chevron sign; and a green, red, and white sign, emblazoned by a dinosaur, for Sinclair gas. I thought of all the people with whom I'd been on the road: all the truckers, all the people who sold me Diet Cokes, the old guy at the gas pump who'd washed my windshield the night before in the town of Beaver; the people who'd made up my bed with fresh sheets, cleaned the shower and laid out towels; who'd taken my credit card, served me coffee, told me where the bathroom was, pointed the way to the ice machine, and told me to drive safely.

I thought of the priests who'd said Mass; the fellow worshipers—whose names I would never know, whose faces I'd already forgotten—who'd sat faithfully beside me in the pews. The friends, old and new, who accepted me the way I was. The family who all my life had loved me in spite of my faults. I'd completed a long, hard trip. I'd gone alone, and I'd endured till the end. I'd gone with Christ, and the angels, and what had happened was sacred and hidden and private, like what happens in a betrothal or a marriage bed.

I got down on my knees and prayed a canticle from the Song of Songs: "O my dove, in the clefts of the rock, in the covert of the cliff, let me see your face, let me hear your voice; for your voice is sweet, and your face is lovely" (9:2). And then I brushed my hair, applied makeup, and in a black muscle shirt, good jeans, and silver earrings, made my way down for (the wretched, free) coffee and got whistled at by an incoming construction worker. For—I could say it at last—in my way, I am actually kind of a babe.

Maybe I wasn't meant to be a nun after all.

Chapter Eight

HUMILITY

Sign of Jonah

In 2010 I gave notice on the L.A. apartment in Koreatown where I'd lived since 1992, disposed or gave away most of my belongings, packed up my car, and took off for an open-ended sabbatical. It was a big move—I didn't know whether or not I'd return—and before I left, my friend Ellen volunteered to let me use her address for forwarding my mail.

Ellen was raised Polish Catholic in Detroit, and she had long since moved on from her roots and from any practice of the faith. Yet she is, in many ways, a far better person than me: honest, generous, decent, and fair. She doesn't gossip and she rarely badmouths, but there are a couple of groups of people for whom she can barely hide her contempt: bum politicians and the Church.

"They won't let 'em use condoms in Africa!" she'd railed on our last hike. "They hate gay people!"

"The Church doesn't hate gay people," I replied weakly. "The Church isn't hoping people die of AIDS. It's acknowledging the power of sex, trying to get across that we miss out on the gift if..."

"They say sex between gay people is a sin. That's not hate? You cannot tell me that the Catholic Church doesn't hate gay people!"

I wanted to say, "I don't go to church for the politics; I go because I'm a sinner myself." I wanted to say, "In all my brokenness and weakness and inadequacy, I love Christ." I wanted to say, "Don't think I don't get that you are in many ways a better 'Christian' than I am." As usual, instead I gave her a pained smile and changed the subject.

And now, three months after that hike, I'd committed to thirty days of silence at a retreat house thousands of miles from L.A., wondering why I'd come. I'd already ordered my life to writing. But I was here to discern: Was that enough? Was there something more that I could/should be doing? Was I called to a deeper surrender—the what, how, and why of which I didn't and might not ever know?

The first time I met with my spiritual director, a man who'd lived in silence for decades, he sat and looked at me and then he asked, "So what did you come to the desert to see?"

I said: "Well, it's been a long journey, geographically and emotionally and spiritually..." And then I bit back tears and proceeded to tell him my life story: the lonely childhood, the twenty years of hard drinking, the difficult marriage, the conversion to Catholicism, the finding of my way to writing, the death of my father, the breast cancer, the divorce, the lifelong pattern of codependency, my recent impulse to pare down, my driving desire to get close to Christ.

To which he said nothing. I don't mean he kept a friendly, respectful silence. I mean he barely moved a facial muscle. I mean he hardly blinked. Finally he said: "Well, the main thing is you want to pray a good three or four hours a day."

I'd just come out of three months of relative solitude at a writer's residency in Taos, New Mexico. I'd been looking forward to this retreat for almost a year, but I soon found that I had no intention of praying, and probably no ability to pray, for any such length of time each day. Still, I did the best I could. I woke and sat in silence for an hour or two: praying the Divine Office, listening. I read. I took notes on what I read. I napped. I wrote. I sat for an hour or two more, looking at the birds. I took long walks.

And though I was happy to be there, and grateful, I had many objections! Oh, there were many reforms I wanted to make! The first thing that made me crazy was the food: fake bread, fake cheese, fake salad dressing. How could people of prayer eat such bad food? I'm as into austerity—maybe more into austerity—as the next person, but would ordering in some fresh, crusty bread, or a decent hunk of cheddar, or some sharp-tasting greens have killed anyone?

The second thing that made me crazy was the Mass. Why did the cross in the chapel where daily Mass was celebrated not have a body on it? Why did we not genuflect upon entering the sanctuary, observe the Sign of Peace, or kneel? Why had the Penitential Rite, the Intercessionary Prayers, the Responsorial Psalm—the Psalms!!!—been excised? Where was the blood, the anxiety, the majesty? The Mass had been sanitized and euthanized. The Mass had been emasculated.

Meanwhile Ellen would forward my mail. Ellen would send batches of homemade chocolate espresso bars, neatly packaged and labeled. One day I received a small, clearly used, hole-punch notebook, bound in black plastic. Stuck to the inside front cover was a turquoise Post-It on which she'd written:

Heath dear—
My 88-year-old Aunt, Sr. Emelita, often gives me stashes
of old notepads and pens. (Usually, the pens don't work).
She gives me old chocolate, too…all the gifts that people

bring nuns. So, I take the notepads and use them. This little notebook spoke to me because I like the little-lined paper. When I got home and looked more closely, I saw she had notes from a retreat almost 20 years ago and it seems fitting to send it to you. Use it. Give it away. Throw it away. Whatever. Love you. Miss you.

Elbow

The first page was headed "Retreat—1992." I began reading, transfixed by the fact that eighteen years before Sr. Emelita had been grappling with the same things I was grappling with now; that an eighty-eight-year-old nun and a fifty-seven-year-old former drunk, ex-lawyer, divorcee, wanderer-seeker-pilgrim could meet in Christ; that in spite of Ellen's and my seemingly divergent views, she had understood that I might find value in this relic.

Three lines, from separate pages, jumped out and instantly assembled themselves into a kind of mantra:

Look for the good in people.

Aging is part of Calvary.

Mary couldn't see the road ahead.

I liked having the notebook nearby. Every time I looked at it, I thought of Sr. Emelita and the mantra. I used the blank pages to keep track of the birds I saw from my porch and on my walks. Scarlet tanager. Scissor-tailed flycatcher. Cedar waxwing. Altamira oriole.

I kept hoping that my spiritual director would be more forth-coming, but as the days rolled by there was nothing from his end *at all*. I sincerely tried to be open and honest: nothing. I told him my heart was burning within me, like the disciples on the road to

Emmaus: nothing. I copped to my pettiness, my irritation, even my concerns about the Mass: nothing.

My "desert" had shaped up to be of a completely different kind than I'd expected. I'd gotten rid of half my belongings, and I wasn't going to get even a drop of water! I'd come hoping for a moment of peace, and I'd been in more or less continual suffering, with no peace, since I arrived. I kept thinking of that passage from the Gospels: "Jesus answered them, 'An evil and adulterous generation asks for a sign, but no sign will be given to it except the sign of the prophet Jonah'" (Matthew 12:40).

The day before I left, I went, one last time, to talk to my spiritual director. There he sat in a long-sleeved plaid shirt, a spidery, hunched-over figure drinking water from a white plastic cup. Six days a week he said noon Mass; Sundays at nine. His was a life the usefulness of which I had always felt I would stake my life on. But what if he had wasted it? What if I were wasting mine?

I thanked him. I said how much I had gotten out of my time there, which was true. I had learned that I was not a hermit. I had learned that I had no special vocation to solitude or prayer. In the oppressive heat, in the gone-wrong silence, in the perceived lack of fellow feeling, I had seen that my place was among people: trudging to Mass; communing with my fellow sober alcoholics and addicts, shoring up my dear, loyal friends—chief among them Ellen—just as they shored up me.

I saw that I had come out to the desert hoping to get closer to God, and God had pried my fingers off him. I had come out, at least in part, hoping to avoid the tension of writing—the sticky arena of self-promotion, the inglorious world of publishing, a culture that values writing, if at all, as a means to become a celebrity, not as a vocation—and the message I'd "heard" was: That tension is your life.

I'd hoped there'd be more. I had hoped to gain a foothold. I had hoped to "hear" something else in the silence.

I packed up my notebooks and icons and bird guides and left the next day. I saw a pair of white-tailed deer on the way out, and the pond with the pale pink lily pads, and a golden-fronted flicker.

"We shed tears because we were given a glimpse of the way life was created to be and is not," wrote Frederick Buechner in *The Longing for Home*.[1]

I pulled out onto the highway.

Look for the good in people.

Aging is part of Calvary.

Mary couldn't see the road ahead.

Chapter | Nine

KINDNESS

Quartzsite

On a road trip several years ago, I got stranded in the dusty desert town of Quartzsite, Arizona. My car had overheated and died on the highway, necessitating a $175 tow charge, an abrupt change in travel plans, and a queasy sense of having dropped down the rabbit hole—possibly forever—into a land of pulsing, mirage-like heat.

While my radiator was being replaced—parts had to be ordered, so this took a couple of days—I holed up at the local Super 8. I was dying to tell someone of my plight, but with no online access, no cell-phone reception, and without a car, Quartzsite was slim pickings. Setting out on a walk the next morning, I discovered the Love's Truck Stop, the Carl's Jr., the Burger King, and the folks hawking minerals, rocks, and crystals—the sun was so hot I burned my fingers on a hunk of quartz—out of the backs of their battered pickups.

Then, making my way down West Main, I stumbled upon what was clearly one of Quartzsite's quirkier establishments. Reader's Oasis Books, a kind of open-air tent fashioned from tarps, screens, and an old shipping container, looked like something a character from *The Treasure of the Sierra Madre* had dreamed up. The mere sight of the place cheered me—but it got better. Ducking inside I was greeted by a fellow who, except for a macramé G-string, several turquoise necklaces, and a palm-leaf Stetson, was entirely nude.

This, I soon learned, was the proprietor of Reader's Oasis for the past sixteen years: Paul Winer. If it were winter, he informed me, he'd be mobbed, selling books to the thousands of snowbirds who pass through each season. In the sweltering summer heat, with business down, he graciously fetched me an ice-cold Diet Coke and gave me the grand tour.

Reader's Oasis was overlain with a pall of pipe-tobacco smoke, neat as a pin, and meticulously arranged into what Paul called "book sculptures." He had sections on ghost towns, mining, railroads, true adventures, and "circus." He had romance, 1950s pulp fiction, a 1941 first edition of the Avon paperback of *Elmer Gantry*, and a shelf of Oprah's picks. "Eighty thousand titles," he reported. "That's different *titles*, not like Barnes & Noble."

Bookstores have always been oases for me. Besides, I was thrilled just to have someone to talk to, especially after my highway scare of the previous day. It was a little strange talking to a sixty-three-year-old man with a bare bum and his genitals in a pouch, but who was I to judge? He'd always been this way, he said—just felt more comfortable without clothes.

As Billie Holiday wafted from the tape deck, he pointed out the mesquite-shaded cactus garden he'd built to the rear of the store, with comfortable chairs for folks to rest in. He showed me a petrified clamshell found in a nearby wash: "Hard to believe," he mused, gazing out at the sunbaked hills, "but this whole place used to be an ocean." He listened to my whole sorry story, and when I told him where my car was, said, "Best Auto? Johnny'll take care of you; don't worry about a thing."

It seemed like a long shot, but, "Do you have any religious stuff?" I asked. A few minutes later, Paul was wrapping up Thomas Merton's *Bread in the Wilderness*: $2.50; the store picked up the tax. Then he refilled my water bottle and offered to let me use his bike for the day. "Thanks anyway," I told him. "But I think I'll keep walking."

Setting out once again, the sun blazing, I thought of stranded travelers, and Good Samaritans, and how someday we'll stand before God naked. I turned around for one last look but—maybe a bend in the road, maybe the heat—Reader's Oasis had vanished.

Chapter Ten

DILIGENCE

The Trial

I used to make ninety bucks an hour doing part-time legal research and writing—work I wasn't crazy about but was grateful for as it supported the creative writing I love. I didn't quite realize how grateful I was, though, until my boss stopped paying me, leaving me $2,817 in the hole with no other means of support.

I'd found the job ten years before by sending out resumes cold to lawyers listed in the Yellow Pages. Prior to that, I'd worked for four years in civil litigation, loathed the incessant, back-biting conflict, and quit to pursue my vocation as a writer. Getting hired as a legal freelancer had seemed like a godsend. I never had to go to court or deal with clients; my boss brought the assignments to, and picked them up from, my door.

My job was to write motions, appeals, and writs: work that was nitpicky, detail-oriented, and boring beyond belief. As a matter of conscience, honor, and professionalism, I prided myself on doing the best job I possibly could, on not padding my hours, on never missing a deadline. Still, litigation, especially after having seen it in practice, struck me as almost intrinsically violent, intrinsically wrong. Far from resolving disputes to anyone's satisfaction, our adversarial system only seemed to breed more enmity, anger, and hurt.

Weeks, then months, drifted by and my boss still hadn't paid me. Even then, though, I didn't want to sue him. He drove me crazy sometimes, but I also kind of liked him. I was proud he thought enough of my work to have kept me on for ten years. We'd fought and made up so many times our "relationship" sometimes felt like an old, battle-scarred marriage. He'd been up to my apartment to shoot the breeze; we'd had a cup of coffee together at my dining room table. I kept remembering the afternoon he'd talked about vacationing in Hawaii, how much he'd liked it: walking along the beach, marveling at the birds.

And so I wheedled, I nagged, I got angry, I offered to set up a payment plan, and the very fact that he seemed impervious to my pleas frustrated me even more. Twenty-eight hundred bucks was for me a huge sum of money, and those thirty-plus hours of drudgery he'd stiffed me for rankled—not least of all because he was a plaintiff's attorney specializing in employment discrimination. Still, there was another reason I didn't want to sue. Unlike my boss, I'd never been cut out to be a trial lawyer. I wanted too much to make everyone happy, I wanted too badly to do a good job. I hated confrontation.

But no matter which way I turned, I couldn't seem to figure out what to do in this situation. I wanted to believe that if you live in honesty and truth, you'll get what's rightfully yours—but that wasn't happening. I wanted to be as harmless as a dove and shrewd as a serpent ("See, I am sending you out like sheep into the midst of wolves; so be wise as serpents and innocent as doves," [Matthew 10:16]), and I was being neither. I wanted to give my boss every chance I could, but I wanted to be a good steward of my money, too—and it was starting to look like one of those things would have to give.

When another couple of months went by and I still hadn't seen a cent, I decided to sue my boss in small-claims court. Deep in my heart, I knew my boss *wanted* to pay me; he just needed a little nudge.

I filled out the forms, schlepped to the downtown courthouse, and paid the fees. It came as a bit of a shock when my boss evaded the first process server—that was fifty-five bucks wasted. For a second $55, the next guy nailed him at the office but then sent back the wrong proof of service form—twice—which meant two extra trips downtown for me. Meanwhile, I spent hours dutifully collating the paperwork. I had copies of my federal and state tax returns, with the most relevant entries highlighted; I had bills for January through December, underlined and asterisked.

The day of the hearing at the downtown superior courthouse, the hall outside Room 541 was packed. Anxiously scanning the crowd, I was thrilled to find my boss apparently wasn't going to show up. I would win by default, and the boss would have to cough up the dough. A clerk named Mike let us in, ordered us to sit down, and barked fifteen minutes of instructions at us. The judge swept to the bench with a look that said, "If you're expecting *People's Court*, you've got another thing coming."

When he called my case, I jumped smartly to my spot. "You did some legal work you didn't get paid for," the judge said. "Do you have an invoice of some kind?" "Yes indeed," I replied eagerly, brandishing an inch-thick sheaf of exhibits bristling with binder clips, tab markers, and Post-its. He regarded me coldly for a moment, then drew back as if from a snake and closed the file. "I hope you can collect your money," he said. "Bowden vs. Flores?" It took me a second to realize I had in fact won by default. That was easy, I thought, gathering up my things and thinking how lovely it would be when I soon received a check for almost three thousand dollars.

Little did I know my boss was just warming up. Three weeks later, he filed a motion for relief, claiming he'd "miscalendared" the earlier hearing. From start to finish, the second hearing was a nightmare. First, the clerk announced that my boss had called to say he'd be a half-hour late. The half hour morphed into an hour and fifteen minutes, during which I fretted that we'd get in trouble or be put last on the list. Then, when he finally did show up, he beckoned me imperiously out to the hallway, ostensibly to exchange exhibits. I followed, and he first ignored me; then stalled, saying he needed more time to get them together; then announced that he'd accidentally brought the wrong ones.

It was when we were finally in front of the judge, though, that my boss delivered the coup de grâce. For that was when he proceeded to claim that the real reason he hadn't paid me was I'd done shoddy work and padded my bill.

I was flabbergasted: My professional pride wounded to the quick, my heart stung by betrayal. "B-but, Your Honor," I stammered, "he always said he just didn't have the money. There's no evidence of any such thing. I'd worked for him for ten years, he'd never once mentioned...."

My boss cut in, sounding calm and reasonable. "Your Honor, I...I trusted Heather, I never had any reason to believe she wasn't billing me fairly. But when I sat down and compared the motion for summary judgment and the appeal in the Hughes case…well, she just copied most of it right in….”

This was such a blatant ploy I could hardly think straight. Any lawyer who specializes in a particular area routinely uses some of the same basic language when drafting motions, appeals and so forth; it would be a complete waste of time—and true bill padding—to start from scratch for every motion.

I looked down at the documents again and then pleadingly back up at the judge. “This is the first time he's raised this argument, Your Honor, and I'm so upset, just being here…. He never showed these to me out in the hallway. Could I have a couple of minutes to sit down and look at them?”

“No,” the judge replied curtly, and swept back into chambers.

Gathering up my things, I could hardly believe the hideous turn things had taken. Maybe I'd been naïve, but I'd thought my boss was my friend. Certainly I'd never thought him capable of looking me in the eye and lying. He'd drunk coffee in my apartment! I'd run out to his double-parked car to pick up files in my pajamas! I'd tried hard to be a good employee; I'd bent over backward to accommodate him. In ten years I'd never once missed a deadline. And now he was not only cheating me; he was accusing me of having cheated *him*!

A week later, the judgment came back for $1,800—a thousand less than what I was owed. I was still smarting over that when my boss *appealed* it. I seriously considered giving up at that point, but then I talked to a friend who'd filed a small-claims case and won, and when her employer had refused to pay, she'd gotten a writ of execution, and the sheriffs had come and put yellow tape around the deadbeat's office and started hauling out his furniture.

I imagined my boss's office door splintered with a battering ram, the files and deposition transcripts scattered all over the floor, the sign on his wall that said "Relax and Let God Do It" broken underfoot. I smiled.

The appeal required proving the case all over again, this time in superior court. Now that I knew the accusations he was going to make, I came to the hearing fully prepared. My boss was late again, and when he appeared this time, it was only to report that he'd "forgotten" his exhibits. The judge was oblivious to these manipulative stalling tactics, which infuriated me. As a consequence my boss, as usual, appeared calm and collected, while I— with every bit of law, spirit, justice, truth, right, and a carefully collated stack of evidence on my side—came off like an hysterical harpy.

But worse than that, while to me my very dignity as a human being was at stake, the judge simply seemed bored.

"Lawyers shouldn't be arguing over 500 dollars," he yawned.

"It's not 500, it's 2800," I quavered bravely, thinking of my recent divorce, my inability to afford health insurance, the $18,000 I'd grossed the year before.

Then, since the poor beleaguered boss had neglected to bring his exhibits, the judge ordered us to come back yet *again* the next day. "Nine-thirty, is that OK for you, Miss King?"

It took everything I had not to scream, "No, it's not OK! He's the one who showed up an hour and a half late without his exhibits! I was here exactly when I was supposed to be—like I have been every other time! Why should *I* have to come back?" Instead I turned on my heel, fighting back tears, and left.

To my horror, my boss followed me out to the hallway.

"Heather?" he asked gently. "Do you want to talk settlement?"

Settlement? I thought. *After you've ripped me off blind? After you've disrespected, my status as a fellow member of our "profession," my womanhood, my humanity?* I whirled around to face him and hissed, "How *dare* you address me," my voice unbelievably, shockingly loud.

The hapless folks trying to eat their lunches on the benches lining the hall froze. "Don't you *ever* try to talk to me again!" I shrieked, and boarded the down escalator, still seething. I just couldn't believe some people didn't think that to be kind and fair and tell the truth mattered. The whole thing made me feel I was crazy, or bad, or dishonest in some secret way unknown even to me.

The next day, the judge listened, bored, to a few more minutes of evidence, then took the case under advisement. Over the weekend, upset as I still was, I thought about how I'd screamed at my boss in the hallway. Turning the other cheek doesn't mean being a doormat, but returning someone else's psychological violence with your own—something Christ never did, even to Judas—wasn't the answer either. Also I kept thinking of those people who'd been quietly eating their lunches; witnessing someone flying into an apoplectic rage was the kind of disturbing scene that would have stayed with a person all day. So Monday I sent my boss another note. "I'm sorry I yelled at you in the hall last week," it said. "I hope you can forgive me."

Tuesday the judgment arrived in the mail for $1,417. So much for justice: On the basis of zero evidence, the amount my boss owed me had been cut in half. He was supposed to either pay up or file a statement of assets within thirty days.

Sure enough, on day thirty-two, I came home to a message on my machine: "Hi, Heather? I'm calling regarding the judgment. I don't have all the money at this time. I was trying to get it all to give to you, but it doesn't look like I'm going to have it for you for another few days, a month or so. I'm hoping I will have *some* money Monday or Tuesday. Talk to you soon."

Talk to me soon: About *what*? The fact that I had won, and he *still* wasn't going to give me the money? My only recourse now was to get a subpoena issued and haul my boss back into court: Having failed to pay up, theoretically he could now be forced to divulge the whereabouts of his assets. A subpoena has to be personally served, however, which meant another trip to the small-claims window—which I made—and another $55 for a process server. They called one morning to say, true to form, they couldn't find him. He was never at home; he was never in his office.

My eyes fell on the crucifix above my desk: the intersection of heaven and earth, the spiritual world and the material world. *What would Jesus do?* I wondered. What kind of look would Jesus have given my boss that first time outside the courtroom: the first time we'd met in months? It wouldn't have been the look I'd given him: a look of reproach, calculated, however unconsciously, to induce guilt. No, Jesus would have had nothing of the victim in him: he would have already absolved the boss, and at the same time he would have called upon him to live up to some level of honesty that, much as I longed to be more spiritually evolved, I couldn't even imagine.

And what kind of look, right now, would Jesus be giving me? A look that said, "You don't have to put yourself through this anymore"? "Your time would be better spent looking for a job."? I probably *should* have been looking for a job, but the issue went deeper than that. I could point the finger at my boss all I wanted, but in a way he had the firmer faith. He believed in the legal system and it was working fine for him. What did I really believe in? Way back at the beginning, I'd said to myself, I'm going to keep praying for him—and then I'm going to sue him. Was it really possible to do both; for a heart to open and close simultaneously?

I thought of that passage in the Bible where Jesus says, "No one can serve two masters; for a slave will either hate the one and love the other, or be devoted to the one and despise the other. You cannot serve God and wealth" (Matthew 6:24), I thought of how wealth isn't just, or necessarily, money: it can be our self-righteousness, our hardened hearts, our willful blindness, our fear.

Here was the real deal: I'd ignored a long, long trail of red flags. I'd always known my boss was sleazy. I'd seen the things he'd done to clients. I'd heard the excuses he me made to judges. For years I'd accepted his excuses to me when he delivered my monthly check late.

My real sin was I'd continued to put myself in harm's way long after I should have known better. My real sin was pride: I'd actually thought if I was a good enough sport and did a good enough job, I could continue in a situation from which I should have removed myself years ago. My real sin was fear: that this was the only job in the world that would allow me to continue to write; that if I quit, I'd never find another.

I'd also never allowed myself to ask, *How loyal an employee could I really have been all those years if I'd been ambivalent about the work?* That didn't mean the boss didn't owe me the money I'd earned. But I was attaching every grievance I'd ever had—against my childhood, the world, God—to this one.

In the end, the legal system does not really address discrimination, or betrayal, or the hurt and anger they give rise to: There's a higher law that does—the healing power of love—and practicing it is the work of a lifetime.

So let it begin with me. Let me start by praying to be more rigorously honest—to myself, to God, to the rest of the world. Let me pray to never again knowingly put myself in a position to be hurt.

And way, way down the line, let me imagine my old boss and me. We're on a beach together in Hawaii, marveling at the birds. He looks into my eyes and says he's sorry. We embrace as brother and sister.

Chapter Eleven

FAITHFULNESS

A Really Dangerous Thing

I find there are two types of people who attack me when they discover I'm Catholic. The first are lapsed or disgruntled Catholics who claim to be revolted by the Church but can't stop talking about it. The second type, the Pharisees, are always trying to get me to say something bad about other (in their eyes, lukewarm) members of the Church. None of these folks can bear the hideous gap between how a follower of Christ should be and how a person who claims to be a follower of Christ actually is.

But you have to be somewhat nuts to sign up for something that is basically impossible to achieve. As Thomas Merton observed: "We must remember that in order to choose religious life, you must be a misfit..."[1]

Christ did not confine himself to politics. He didn't say, "We need more rights." He didn't say, "Let's overthrow the Romans." He said, "We need to live in total integrity and love. In order to do so, we need a Church, and because we are never going to do so perfectly, the Church will inevitably also be imperfect."

To avoid the scandal of the cross, which is in some sense to say the scandal of the Church, is impossible. How could a Church made up of us be anything but imperfect? What Church would take us except a Church that tolerated imperfection? Where else would we drag ourselves to pray for the people we resent at any given moment—our mothers, our spouses, our kids, our friends, our politicians, the other people in church—but to church? Where else would we go to be reminded of the perpetual death and perpetual rebirth but to Mass? In order to try resurrecting the Church we keep wrecking, we have to keep going to church—because we need Christ: to walk with us, to live.

Religion doesn't mean acting better than other people; it means, if we're lucky, getting to act a little better than we used to ourselves. As the writer Madeleine L'Engle observed: "We do not draw people to Christ by loudly discrediting what they believe, by telling them how wrong they are and how right we are, but by showing them a light that is so lovely that they want with all their hearts to know the source of it."[2]

You can't do that if you're driven by anger or fear. You have to have some kind of joy. And this seems to require looking at our darkest wounds: our resentments, our seemingly hard-wired patterns, neuroses, fears. The things we're ashamed of, the things we're guilty about, the compulsive patterns we can't shake free of, no matter how hard we try. That to me is the real challenge of Christ, and what sets me on fire about the Gospels.

We all want to learn compassion, but as we go about trying to be of service to the world, we are going to uncover some very difficult truths, about ourselves, about others. And that's what we have to work through. That's the hard stuff, the hardest stuff there is. Family stuff. Sex stuff. Our identity as a person who has a certain kind of career, or a certain political leaning. Our reputation in the community, perhaps. We may decide to give up certain things, maybe many things, out of love. Money, maybe; sex for a time, maybe forever. But that's where the joy comes in.

The politicians tell us that our enemies are dangerous, terrorists are dangerous, people who don't support the United States are dangerous, but the really dangerous idea is the Gospels. Dangerous because you consent to be not useful, to not be productive, to not be relevant. Dangerous because you never know whether you have staked your life, or whether you're a sham and a coward. Dangerous because you offer up your entire self and you're no better or kinder, no less petty or more generous, no more effective, squared away, or "together" than when you began. You're more crushed, uncertain, and vulnerable. You're more human. That's the good news—but to be human is a perilous, perilous undertaking.

We are all just here with our broken, shattered hearts, hoping against hope for the Second Coming and trying to not kill ourselves or each other before it arrives. Expending our entire strength to eke out the tiniest act of kindness. Rolling our rock, with Sisyphus, up a mountain whose top we're never going to reach. Knowing that in the end we die alone and praying to be stand-up enough, just once or twice in our lives, to comfort someone else who is dying, as Christ comforted the Repentant Thief who was nailed to the cross beside him.

That's faith. That's the Resurrection.

As Thérèse of Lisieux neared the end of her life, her older sister Céline, frustrated at having so much less charity than she would have liked, exclaimed, "Oh, when I think how much I have to acquire!"

"Rather," Thérèse replied, "how much you have to lose."[3]

Chapter Twelve

PRUDENCE

Sanctuary

I'm not sure what I pictured when I decided to make a retreat at an unfamiliar monastery, but it wasn't this: a jumble of outbuildings and abandoned sheds, piles of barrels draped with blue tarps, a labyrinth of dirt roads. I circle around a couple of times, spot a sign saying "Registration" in the window of the bookstore, and park. After eight hours on the road, I'm hoping to be greeted by some calm, prayer-centered soul. Instead a heavily made-up woman named Dot startles, turns down the volume on an Amy Grant tape, and flutters nervously around trying to find someone to replace her at the cash register.

We walk the few hundred yards to a barracks-like structure and she ushers me into Room 1. I do a quick inventory—two twin beds, midget bed-stand, broken Venetian blinds. "There's no... desk?" I venture.

Dot's rolling eyes say it all: *There's always gotta be one, doesn't there?* she's thinking. "If I could make a suggestion," she says tightly, "next time you go on a retreat, you might want to inform the people of your needs beforehand," as if a desk were a piece of esoteric equipment; as if I'd asked for something outlandish, like a pack of condoms.

All the next day the retreat master, Jim, an overweight pecan farmer with a John Deere cap, makes hourly progress reports on his painstaking, convoluted attempts to locate a desk. Finally one of the monks approaches me in chapel, looks furtively around, as if we were planning a tryst, and whispers, "We've finally found you another room. Room 12."

And the kicker is, when I go over to look at it, Room 12 doesn't have a desk either—at which point I realize Room 1 is fine. Room 1 is wonderful. Hot water, heat, an outlet for my laptop, a porch.

Out back, I saw a beautiful orange bird this morning. There are cottonwoods and cholla, and a little stream running through.

* * *

I'm here because I need a break from my life—the book nobody wants to buy, the one-bedroom apartment where I write, my husband Tim, the early stage breast cancer I found out about last year and decided to treat with surgery only. "Oh, you're using holistic medicine," people say approvingly. But I am not using holistic medicine. I am not seeing an acupuncturist, a nutritionist, an herbalist; I am not taking vitamin supplements or Laetrile or mistletoe tea. Aside from cutting down on fat, I am doing pretty much what I was doing already, which is eating healthily, walking, writing, praying, and hanging out with other sober people.

But you got cancer doing that, I can hear people thinking. So I got cancer! People get cancer, they die from cancer. My problem is not cancer; it's lack of faith, a lack of acceptance, living in illusion. That's the real reason I'm here.

This big place is apparently run by six or seven monks, all of whom appear to be in the throes of deep spiritual crisis. The Divine Office—Vigils, Lauds, Vespers, Compline—is the heart of Benedictine spirituality. At every other monastery I've attended, it's prayed with the utmost attention and reverence. Here the monks show up looking like they just crawled out of bed; they slump and slouch and scratch and yawn; they seem crabby and bored. One, a sixtyish fellow with bloodshot eyes, practically lies down in his seat after quavering the entrance antiphon; another, a tall, rawboned youth with hacked-off hair, crosses his legs, gazes out the window and dangles his breviary in one hand. This, it turns out, is the abbot.

I was appalled for about ten seconds and then I realized that I am so clueless and broken right now that I feel much more at home with these folks than I would with people who were reverent and assured.

* * *

For the last three years, I've given up coffee for Lent, and I'm preparing to do so again this year, after the retreat is over on Ash Wednesday. A hundred times a day, I contemplate how horrible this will be. Here is the extent of my caffeine addiction: For the last two mornings, I've woken before dawn and driven fifteen miles to the local Circle K for a jumbo "Dark Roast." It would be one thing if the coffee were actually good, but it barely has an edge on the watered-down swill they serve in the dining hall.

Still, knowing myself, I will make the trek to Circle K every morning during the retreat.

* * *

I've figured out how the monks keep the place up and running: the army of oblate volunteers who spend the winter in a nearby RV park. The first night I met a retired couple named Fran and Earl, who immediately informed me they'd been coming here for eleven years. The next night I met Lois and Vern. "Oh I met a nice couple last night who do the same thing you do," I told Vern.

"Fran and…." "We've been coming here twelve years," he cut in. "They've only been coming eleven."

For once, in chapel this morning, I was actually able to attend to the meaning of the psalms and readings. I've been praying the Divine Office on my own for two years, but usually I'm still so self-conscious, so eager to "progress," that I never get around to orienting myself toward Christ; I make it all about me. I keep doing it because I figure it's pleasing to God; because maybe after thirty or forty years, I'll be purified; because there's only one way to make it be about Christ: to keep on praying. And in the meantime, every once in a blue moon, it is like it was this morning.

* * *

One of the RV women is in charge of cooking, and her approach seems to be to take a food and smother it with so much fat that it is unrecognizable not only as the food it was, but as any food at all. Last night dinner consisted of pork chops in an inch of greasy breading, a string-bean casserole enhanced with suet, and a tray of deep-fried, syrup-drenched apple fritters that must have weighed a pound-and-a-half apiece.

I happened to be sitting at the same table as the chef, and it came out in the course of the conversation that she makes a special "black bread" for Ash Wednesday (they serve only bread and water that day). "What's in it?" I piped up eagerly, hoping it might by accident contain a stray nutrient or two.

"Oh they've begged me for the recipe," she replied coyly, "but I won't give it to them. Four Seasons wanted the ranch dressing recipe from my restaurant, too, but I wouldn't give that out either"

I don't know what horrified me more: that she had been

connected in any way with the operating of a restaurant, or that she imagined I might want to duplicate anything she had cooked.

* * *

There's a nun here from Baltimore, about my age, named Georgina, who has breast cancer and leukemia. They give her five years, tops, she told me last night. I might drive her into town to get some supplies as she is constipated, exhausted from radiation and, like me, having a hard time with the food. At dinner, I saw her give a big smile to Jim, the retreat master who I'd decided I didn't like, or who didn't like me. Constantly, I am reminded of my meanness.

* * *

Last night I skipped dinner and went to the chapel for Compline at 8:30—pitch black outside, freezing cold—but they must have already had it in the dining hall because nobody was there. So I went to the Lady of Guadalupe alcove, where the light was, and said Evening Prayer by myself, and then sat by the Blessed Sacrament for a while. That once sounded so hokey to me: the Adoration of the Blessed Sacrament. Now I see it as a deep, mysterious gift. What solace, what peace to sit with him, the Great Physician, the Master Anesthesiologist.

I kept thinking today of last Sunday's reading from Ecclesiasticus: "When a sieve is shaken, the refuse appears; so do a person's faults when he speaks" (27:4). Or acts. Giving Sister Georgina a ride into town this afternoon, I saw myself through her eyes. First, she was embarrassed to be going out with me, as any retreatant worth his or her salt apparently does not leave the grounds for the duration of the retreat, while I have gone on my lame coffee runs every morning. Second, she wanted to pick up some juice and tea because she's sick: I wanted to pick up some chocolate and a last coffee before Lent begins tomorrow.

To top it all off, I repaired to my room afterward and proceeded to eat the entire giant Cadbury bar I had purchased at the Safeway, while Georgina was loading up on apricot nectar and chamomile. This was after I judged everyone else for being fat. It doesn't matter where I am, my faults will be revealed.

* * *

My last day on retreat is Ash Wednesday. When I go into the dining hall, each table is bare except for a loaf of dark rustic bread—the secret recipe!—and a white crockery bowl filled with dirt and stones.

At noon Mass, the abbot talks in his homily about prayer as a method of detaching from thought. He observes that one way to do this is to sit in silence with a sacred word. The word many of the monks use, he says, is the Aramaic *Maranatha*: "Come, Lord Jesus." The chapel is packed and, for a second, I wonder if this Middle America parish is ready for contemplative prayer. And then I realize that this whole place probably operates on nothing but prayer, that I know nothing about prayer.

"Remember you are dust, and to dust you shall return," he says afterward, over and over again, as we file up to have our foreheads anointed with ashes.

I spend the afternoon packing and, when Vespers is over, wander behind the chapel, skirt the duck pond, and find my way to the outdoor Stations of the Cross. Like the Adoration of the Blessed Sacrament, the Stations have always struck me as slightly musty and old-school, but someone has put a lot of thought into designing these—I know from the brochure that they incorporate natural features of the landscape—and it seems like a fitting way to end my visit.

I start at Station 1—Jesus is Condemned to Death—noticing a nearby creosote. "This desert bush," the placard reads, "forced to survive with so little water, reminds us of how Jesus felt as he stood before his merciless accusers." I pause to reflect on this happy thought for a minute, then make my way around a boulder to Station 2—Jesus Bears His Cross: "This heavy stone, an impossible burden, is like the cross Jesus was forced to carry to Mount Calvary."

The path winds up a hill; I trudge on, the sun sinking in a pool of red. Station 3—Jesus Falls for the First Time. Station 4—Jesus Meets His Mother. Station 10—Jesus Is Stripped of His Garments: "The spines in this ancient cactus remind us of the Crown of Thorns Jesus wore; of the many humiliations we, too, suffer in our lives." Station 12—Jesus Dies on the Cross: "Just as the trunk of this burned-out tree is stripped bare, so we will be stripped of everything: property, success, looks, health."

And suddenly I am weeping, weeping for the old men and the abused children, for the people so alone they never get prayed for, for Sister Georgina, for myself. I've tried so hard to "get it" by being good: praying the "right" way, giving up coffee, being mature and responsible and accepting about my cancer. But nobody ever "gets" it.

It's not about being good; it's about being vulnerable. It's not about being perfect; it's about becoming human. It's not about pretending that cancer doesn't suck in every possible way; it's about consenting to bear my suffering in a desperate, keening, crawling-on-bloody-knees kind of love for my brothers and sisters, just as, in some mysterious way, my brothers and sisters bear their suffering for me.

Christ wasn't mature and responsible and accepting when they drove the nails through his precious hands, his beautiful sacred feet. He knew the worst spiritual anguish any person can know: "Father, Father, why have you forsaken me?" And yet he doesn't forsake us; he never forsakes us. That's what the resurrection— that light way in the distant future, after these seven dark weeks of Lent—tells us. And I suddenly realize something else: The fact is, I've been jealous of the RVers. They have each other, a community. The fact is I'm terrified of being abandoned myself.

The dinner bell rings and I salivate: I've been fasting all day. Tomorrow I'll leave the silence and the cottonwoods and the birds, and make the long drive home. But for now it's time to walk through the gathering dusk and join the others: the young monks and the old; Dot, Jim, Sister Georgina; Fran and Earl, Lois and Vern, the woman in charge of cooking.

To bow our heads. To eat the good black bread.

Chapter Thirteen

JOY

Copa de Oro

The newscasters make it sound as if nobody walks in Los Angeles—it's too dangerous, too smoggy, too inconvenient—but this is not true. I walk almost every day.

When I lived in Koreatown, I would walk from Hobart and 9th, north to Melrose, east to Vermont, south to Pico. I walked past the grand old apartment buildings: the Gaylord, the Talmadge, the Ancelle. They had slate roofs, scrollwork around the windows, friezes of Egyptian mummies around the top stories. They survived white flight, then black flight, and back in the mid-90s, they had blue banners slung across the corners that said in large block letters: Se Renta—$395.00.

I lived in one of these buildings myself, a beautifully preserved French Normandy: the nicest apartment I'd ever had. It had high ceilings, crown moldings, hardwood floors, and hand-painted tile in the bathroom. It had a formal dining room with a chandelier, a living room with a bank of windows from which white gauze curtains billowed in the breeze, a balcony that overlooked the flower-filled courtyard.

Out on the sidewalk, women pushing wheeled carts sold *elote*—ears of corn dipped in an industrial-size plastic jar of mayonnaise—and men sold *paletas*, the Mexican version of Popsicles. Vehicles were double and triple parked; drug deals were always going down. With the sun on my neck, I would walk past a *copa de oro*—cup of gold—whose trumpet-shaped flowers, pale yellow streaked with amethyst, were so voluptuous I had to restrain myself from biting them.

Back then, I often wondered why I continued to live in this neighborhood. It wasn't because I was poor. Part of the reason I moved to Koreatown in the first place was because I had made a conscious decision—the kind of decision truly poor people never have the luxury of making—to lower my expenses so I wouldn't have to work at a job that was killing me. On the other hand, I was not exactly rich, either, and while I was consequently never quite sure who was "us" and who was "them," perhaps that was not precisely the point. Perhaps the point was realizing that all of us in that neighborhood were connected to one another so closely that everything we did or said or thought radiated out, in some unimaginably mysterious way, to the whole world.

One winter night I walked the half-mile to St. Basil's on Wilshire Boulevard for five o'clock Mass. When I came out, it was getting dark. Between the columns of buildings and the rows of swaying palm trees silhouetted in the dusk, the sun was setting in a blaze of gold. I walked south on Harvard, hedged with red bottlebrush, and turned right on 8th. They were turning on the neon signs in the sushi joints, the billiard halls, the clubs that advertised happy hours. They were turning on the neon signs that glowed from the roofs of the grand old apartment buildings.

I headed south and walked past one of them. Here, too, the lights were coming on. Each window was a frame: a woman standing at an ironing board, a shirtless man shaving, children eating dinner. The air was heavy with the perfume of frying oil and chiles, onions, meat.

I was almost home. Dog droppings littered the mangy strip of grass between the sidewalk and the street. In the gutter lay flyers for cheap auto insurance, an empty box of Cheez-Its, cardboard Big Gulp cups. And up the street, in the gathering dusk, a bunch of Korean girls were shouting and laughing. They had tied together pieces of the kind of white elastic that holds up pajama bottoms and stretched it around saplings and stakes. They were playing Chinese jump rope, and the knowledge that life is everlasting swelled within me.

That was the real reason I continued to live in Koreatown, because my neighbors gave me faith that when we had finished shooting and starving and aborting each other, when there was nothing left to drink or snort or smoke or inject, when we had paved it all over and used it all up and nuked what was left to kingdom come, out of the smoking rubble would rise a woman pushing a baby stroller, a man tinkering with an engine, a geranium growing on a windowsill in an old tin can.

I walked up the steps to my apartment. Through the wrought-iron gate lay the courtyard with its box hedges and calla lilies and moth-eaten roses. From the standard of a carriage lamp, bamboo chimes clacked delicately, like the bones of children. My apartment was on the right-hand side, in the back, upstairs. A light shone in the window. I walked toward it.

Chapter Fourteen

UNDERSTANDING

Irene

On one of my cross-country road trips, I once stayed at the Holy Spirit Monastery in Conyers, Georgia. The retreat house had shared bathrooms, and in spite of my daily devotions—the Divine Office, a nightly examination of conscience, the Jesus Prayer—I almost instantly conceived a violent resentment against the person with whom I shared mine. She was with a church group, and I so had her pegged. Blond perm, suburban, a spiritual lightweight: just the sort who'd go on retreat with people. I, a true pilgrim, was alone: draped head to toe in my usual black, weeping and praying over the mysteries of suffering, meaning, love.

The monks at Holy Spirit are Trappists, gathering in the church at intervals throughout the day to chant the psalms and pray. The entire monastery goes to bed at 8:00 P.M. so as to rise in time for the first office of the day: Vigils at 4:00 A.M. The first night I went to bed at 8, too, only to be jolted awake a few hours later by the sound of explosively loud water pipes: my bathroom-mate was taking a shower and I swear stayed in there past midnight, brushing her teeth, drying her hair.

She was chatty, too, though we were supposed to be keeping silence. When I ran into her the next morning, she launched into a long-winded story about the fact that she didn't have an alarm clock and her girlfriend had lent her one and all she could say was this was her first retreat and it sure was *a learning experience.* Then off she went with her social butterfly friends—Mass at 7:00 A.M., Vespers at 5:20 P.M.: Every time I went to church, she had the nerve to be there, too!

Still, the homily the first day at Mass was about the value of the small act: the smile, the kind word, refraining from the harsh retort. So at dinner, when I found myself in line with her and she started chatting again, I mustered all my spiritual strength and bestowed a small, forbearing smile upon her before I went my way.

The second night she was at it again: flushing the toilet, running the sink. I slept fitfully and at 3:30 A.M. went downstairs for coffee. There she was, sitting in the semi-dark, all perky in a bright, flowered dress and—just as I could have predicted—raring to talk.

"My husband was just diagnosed bipolar and he refuses to admit it," she announced. "'Nothin' wrong with me'," he told the doctor, 'I'm just here for Irene.'"

"Oh," I said, groping for the sugar, "that's hard."

"I'm Polish," she went on. "My mother was in Poland when the Nazis started rounding up people and they put her in an internment camp. You know what she used to tell me? 'When everything is taken from you, you still have your faith.'"

"I guess that's true," I replied.

"Yup, Mom was my odometer. Didn't seem fair when she got Alzheimer's, but God rest her soul, I nursed her through."

Suddenly, I saw my bathroom-mate and myself through God's eyes: she, cheerful in spite of her suffering; me, a self-pitying crab.

"I just joined the praise group at my parish," she went on.

"Right now I'm praying for all the souls in inner turmoil, that they may find comfort and peace."

I thought of myself, fuming on my bed.

"Thank you, Irene," I said, laying a hand on her shoulder.

"Don't mention it," she replied. "That's just me."

Chapter Fifteen

CHARITY

Do This in Memory

That Christ had a preference for the poor was no accident. Like the mysteries of the cross and resurrection, the poor make us feel uncomfortable and awkward; they resist all our efforts to categorize and romanticize them. The poor challenge us in ways we cannot control or predict.

Take Clarence, for instance, the fiftyish panhandler who hangs out at the church where I attend Mass. Once you know who he is and what he wants—once, in other words, you've made "friends" with him—Clarence is way too cool to actually ask for money. He leans against the building reading a paperback or smoking with his long piano player's fingers—his mere presence is supposed to inform you he's in need.

I often give Clarence a dollar or two, but it's usually with a certain measure of unease. He dresses better than I do—not that this is saying much—and he looks and sounds like he could easily get a job if he made the effort. But of course you never know, and then it drives me nuts that he drives me nuts. What do I want him to do? Grovel? Dress in rags? Hand me an affidavit confirming that he lives below the poverty level?

Clarence forces me to face the uncomfortable fact that my giving might derive not so much from compassion as from the need to feel satisfied that my donation is fulfilling an "authentic" need.

But worse than that, he makes me feel like I might be a chump. The poor are not supposed to make us feel like chumps.

Which is why, one recent afternoon when I was heading into church for five o'clock Mass, I wasn't thrilled when Clarence ambled out from the shadows to meet me. For one thing, it was raining and just getting dark out and I didn't much feel like stopping. For another, I find parting with any amount of money deeply painful. Still, Clarence was waiting, one eyebrow cocked, and I'd been avoiding him for the last few days. I quickly tried to extract a single dollar bill from my wallet, but it was clumped together with another, and, afraid of looking stingy, I forked over both. "Thanks, sweetheart," he said, palming them expertly, his voice smooth as silk, his hand already gliding into a pocket, secreting it away with the rest of his stash.

"What is it about him that makes me feel cheap even when I'm giving him money?" I mused as I entered the church. I was still smarting with a vague sense of resentment when, settling into my pew, I sensed a presence at my elbow, a murmuring voice. I glanced over to find a young man kneeling in the aisle. His bottom lip was an erupted ridge of sores oozing yellow liquid, and his fingernails were yellow, too, long and caked with greasy dirt.

I would like to report that the first thought that sprang to my mind was: *Wonderful! A second opportunity to give!* Instead, with all my usual generosity and patience, the words that came up, rather bitterly, were: *Not another one.* I actually considered explaining that I had already done my duty, given not one, but two dollars just moments before to another needy person, but one look at his nakedly pleading face told me that wasn't going to quite cut it.

I expected him to make the usual impersonal request for spare change. Instead, to my horror, he reached into the pocket of his jacket, produced a sheaf of grimy photographs and held the top one up to my face. I saw a tall, smiling boy in front of a shack, a girl with bare arms and a pink dress standing beside him. "This one here's when I was a teenager," he explained eagerly, pointing, "and that's my sister and..."

"Do you need money?" I interrupted, helplessly, redundantly. Of course he needed money—he wouldn't have been on his knees showing a total stranger his family photographs if he didn't need money—but I couldn't bear to hear any more, couldn't bear his vulnerability, couldn't bear that he thought I'd be interested in his memories. I fumbled with my wallet and handed him a dollar, praying he'd move on to someone else and that would be the end of it.

Instead, he held the bill between two fingers and regarded it sadly, quizzically, as if I hadn't grasped the situation at all, as if he'd asked for a coat and I'd given him a button. Then he put his hands together and broke out in a kind of hymn. "Oh, I'm so cold, I'm from Alabama," he said. "Could you help me find my way home, miss? I'm hungry and I'm so cold." His sneakers, caked with mud, stuck out into the aisle, his long, dirty thumb-nail held the sheaf of photos in place, his scabby lips trembled, his dark eyes were pools of suffering.

Those eyes indicted me: in my hand, the wallet felt heavy and hot, a burning coal. If Clarence raised one set of questions, this man raised another. When I gave Clarence money, at least I had the satisfaction of knowing he'd go out and buy a pack of ciga-rettes or a bottle of malt liquor he could enjoy, but this man gave me the feeling that I could empty out my wallet, invite him home, feed him, wash him, give him a blanket, buy him a plane ticket home and none of it would make a particle of difference. He so clearly illustrated the futility of eradicating poverty in general or even the suffering of one person in particular that it seemed as if anything I gave him would be literally like throwing it down a gutter.

Still, he was crouching in the aisle, his dark eyes boring into mine. I extracted a ten from my wallet, half of my heart breaking for him and his pitiful pile of photographs, the other half begrudging, counting the cost. "Oh, thank you, miss," he said, gazing at the bill in wonder, "thank you," and disappeared into the shadows.

I give money to panhandlers all the time, and panhandlers are far from the only "poor" I encounter in my daily life, but something about this man particularly struck me. Maybe it was the fact that he and Clarence were so totally different—had it been fair, for instance, to have given him ten dollars and Clarence only two?—that it jarred me into seeing how I so often lump the people I encounter on the street together into one faceless mass. Maybe it was that I usually give panhandlers one or two dollars, five at the most, that made that ten dollars act like a kind of yeast; I thought of the man to whom I had given it all through Mass.

He was like a koan, the paradoxical riddles used to train Zen Buddhist monks to detach from their dependence upon reason and help them reach "enlightenment." Should I have felt guilty for not having given more—because in my wallet I had more, quite a bit more—or grateful that, with God's help, I had given tenfold what I'd planned on? Did I take the easy way out by giving him money? Should I instead have said, "Okay, let's go have a coffee and chat.

Tell me about your pictures. When's the last time you talked to your sister? Do you want to use my nail file?" Had I really helped? Assuming the bus trip hadn't been a big scam, assuming he ever got there at all, wouldn't he be just as miserable and lost back in Alabama as he was now? Why did I feel so ashamed? Why did I feel so moved?

I pondered these questions all through Mass, one ear on the liturgy, one eye on the carving of the crucified Christ above the altar. I did not come up with any answers, but I did start to see this: Christ is not an idea, a theory, a program; not an answer but an inexhaustible question. Christ is not "the poor." He is all of us, with all of our triumphs and traumas, our weaknesses and strengths, our hopes and our fears. He is Clarence, with his dreadlocks and smirk; he is me clutching my wallet, the man in the aisle with his hand outstretched, the answer to whether the space between us is going to bind us together or keep us apart, the measure of my sin in what I have done, and in what I have failed to do.

If the poor make us feel awkward and confused, perhaps that is exactly the point. We are supposed to give not because it makes sense, but just because it is foolish, just because there are no rules to prevent us from feeling like chumps or misers, just because there is no guarantee the people to whom we give aren't going to go out and buy a hunk of crack or a six-pack or a gun, just because it is never, ever enough. We are supposed to give because the very imperfection of our efforts makes us participants in the nakedness and vulnerability of the crucifixion. We are supposed to give not so much because giving necessarily changes the people to whom we give, but because it changes us.

All during Mass, I continued to think of that young man with the suffering eyes. I thought of his sister's pink dress shimmering in the sun, smelled the honeysuckle in the front yard of the little wooden house they were standing in front of in the picture. Nothing had "happened" in that thirty-second encounter except that a stranger had made me see him as a human being. I can still see him now. I scanned the back of the church when Mass was over, but he had already disappeared.

When I left, there was a third panhandler standing outside, a man in his twenties with dirty blond hair and a rain tunic fashioned from a plastic trash bag. It was dark by then. A drizzle was falling, the rain slanting down in the pool of light where he stood, wordlessly holding out a Styrofoam cup. We parishioners streamed by, averting our eyes. Not a single person stopped. I got in my car and sat watching in the rearview mirror until everyone had come out. He was still standing there, alone in the rain, when the light above the door of the church went dark.

Chapter Sixteen

TEMPERANCE

Mother Teresa

I recently stumbled upon an exhibit, at the L.A. Central Library, by the photographer Yousaf Karsh (1908–2002). I'd not known of Karsh before this nor, to my knowledge, of his black-and-white gelatin prints from the '40s and '50s: beautifully lit, richly textured. Still, I instantly recognized many of the portraits: Ernest Hemingway in a stout wool turtleneck. Winston Churchill, commanding, sardonic. Picasso, with his piercing eyes and a painting of a nude.

They were different faces—elegant faces, handsome faces, intelligent faces—and yet, as I made the rounds of the two rooms that comprised the exhibit, I began to see that in a way, they were the same face. Jacqueline Kennedy: nubile, dewy. Albert Einstein and his leonine white mane. Even Anna Magnini, defeated, oozed sex appeal. These were celebrities whose expressions spoke of vacation homes and domestic help, whose hands toyed with cigarettes, who had made scientific discoveries and waged wars and presided over opulent drawing rooms. "Yes, I'm admired, fawned over, and you can well see why!" many of their eyes seemed to say. Part of me wished I were one of them.

One photo alone stood out. One face so distinguished itself that I stopped short: the face of a small, old, deeply wrinkled, resolutely plain—and by plain I don't mean without depth—woman, her head swathed to mid-eyebrow in a white muslin scarf. Her gnarled fingers gripped a rosary. She looked exhausted, possibly ticked off. Her face was not one any of us, no matter how passionately we admired her work, would have asked for. Her face was a scandal: naked, almost ugly—the face of a woman, we know now, who for fifty years had cried out in spiritual hunger and never heard an answer; who for fifty years had lived in darkness.

It was the face of a woman who had squandered her youth, her sexuality, her capacity for romance on cleaning the sores of lepers and sponging the foreheads of the dying. It was the face of a woman who understood that our task on earth is not to be effective, but to love; that the goal is not success, but love; who knew the terrible cost of love. It was a face that pointed not to itself, but beyond itself: to the Person who transcends the human body and is incarnated in every cell of the human body. It was the face of a woman who had been praised for caring for the dying, and knew all praise goes to God; and who had also been the target of scorn and contempt, for there are those who find cleaning the sores of the sick and sponging the foreheads of the dying cause not for praise, but for rage.

"Why don't you *eliminate* suffering?" such people rail. "If you cared, you'd build better hospitals and *eradicate* suffering! Why do you sit around holding people's hands when you could use your money to start social programs and distribute condoms and support science, politic candidates, technology?" They are really railing against a God in whom they profess not to believe: against reality. And because suffering—ours, theirs, anyone else's—will never, in this world, be eradicated, the effort to comfort, to sit by without fixing, seems stupid and futile. The solution instead seems to be to prevent people from being born, or to get rid of the ones who are in the way, in pain; to be sensible, to sanitize, to clean up.

One person who believed in such "progress," in cleaning things up, was Christopher Hitchens, who would write a book about the woman in the photo calling her a fanatic, a fundamentalist, and a fraud: not because she stole money from her hospices, not because she did anything other than exactly what she claimed to do, not because she was anyone other than exactly who she claimed to be, but because she did not promote abortion.[1]

Other charges were leveled by Hitchens—that she accepted dirty money, that she supported the Duvaliers, the corrupt Haitian dictators (whether or not the charges are true I can't say). But her most egregious offense, according to Hitchens, was that she did not promote abortion: that through her work with the dying, she had come to believe ever more deeply that all life is a sacrament, from its first moments to its last. What incensed Hitchens was the notion that true progress would perhaps lie in becoming mindful of and responsible for our own capabilities of bringing life into the world, and in cherishing life in any tiny way we can, and in learning that to cherish is a crucible.

I looked around at the other photos—so seductive, so attractive—then back at the one before me. I thought, *Perhaps truth is not always, at first glance, beauty. Perhaps truth lies in a light so harsh it scalds our eyes and hearts. Perhaps we need to put our faith in something other than the things the world tantalizes us with and withholds, and every so often gives, and the minute we do get, fill us with terror; for the things of this world don't last. We lose the things of this world— youth, people; our audiences, our homelands—or they are taken from us, and coming to grips with that is another kind of crucifixion.*

Mother Teresa's was a face demanding that we look, finally, upon the least among us, who are a bother and a reproach, and whose suffering haunts us, and whose suffering continues not because we lack social programs, or scientific advances, or literary or theological wit, but because very few have the strength to bear the shame of failure, of ineffectiveness.

Very few of us possess the moral rigor and intellectual honesty to admit that we are all complicit in the suffering of the world. Very few of us have the *duende*—a Spanish term, often applied to bullfighters, meaning, roughly, soul, crossed with class, crossed with sublime, almost insane, bravery—to endure the tension of working to the limit of our emotional, physical, and spiritual strength while never quite knowing whether we are fools to believe that our work is bearing fruit; whether our efforts to joyfully participate in the sorrows of the world matter; whether—one day—Christ will come again.

Mother Teresa's was the face of a woman whose eyes were difficult to read, fathomless, as if behind them burned an unseen light: not a soft glow but a fierce, blistering, scorching conflagration of a light that had been endured for a lifetime—for two thousand years—in silence. It was the face of a woman who had so loved the poor that, at last, she became one of them.

I peered more closely and saw my own face reflected in the glass—aging, alone—a cross hanging from my neck.

Chapter Seventeen

PATICE

PATIENCE

Metaxu

Two prisoners whose cells adjoin communicate with
each other by knocking on the wall. The wall is the thing
which separates them but it is also their means of commu-
nication. It is the same with us and God. Every separation
is a link.[1]

—SIMONE WEIL

When I first met Fred I didn't know he'd be a thorn in my side
for twenty years. I didn't fully know yet what Dostoevsky meant
when he characterized love as "harsh and dreadful" in his book
The Brothers Karamazov. I didn't know yet that the parts of us
that are the most painful, the most difficult, the least susceptible
to healing are the very parts that bind us most closely to others.

Fred and I are both ex-drunks who met trying to stay sober.
Drinking or not, alcoholics can be challenging: touchy; insecure;
charming one minute, sociopathic the next. I'm no exception
(God knows), and neither is Fred. The first time I gave him a ride
home, he complained the whole way—the shyster landlord, the
Filipino "butt-pirate" (Fred's term for a homosexual male) who
cut his hair—then, when I dropped him off, said "Thanks, angel,
that was reaaaaal nice." I've been stuck with him ever since.

Ours is an unlikely friendship. I live to read; Fred cracks a
book maybe once a year. I eat polenta; he eats frozen pizza. Fred

has little use for what he calls "the hipster crowd." Anything "artsy-fartsy," wacked-out, criminally insane, or unneighborly: "Welcome to L.A." Anything you have to lose, yield, or let go of: "Goodbye, Arizona." Every Veterans' Day: "All gave some and some gave all," coupled with a half-hour harangue on the Commies at Social Security, the morons at Medicare, and the crooks in the White House.

Over the years he's suffered a series of illnesses that would have felled an ox, never mind a guy who, before he got sick, weighed maybe 140. He's gone from occasional visits to the Hollywood Presbyterian ER, to frequent stays in whatever ICU will take him, to the board-and-care section of the VA Hospital in West Los Angeles where one more time, he's asked me to visit, and today, one more time, I've come.

The lobby smells of hot lunch food and urine. The Coke machine is busted. I find Fred in his second-floor room standing with his back to the door, hunched over, his head sunk, sucking on his breathing apparatus: a T-shaped contraption of clear plastic that produces clouds of, paradoxically, what looks like smoke, though smoking—along with the Hep-C, the infections on both lungs, and the old bronco-riding fractures—is more or less what's killing him.

"Come in, come in, there's a chair by the window," he coughs. "Want an Ensure?"

Back in the day, Fred for a time worked as a Marlboro man and he hasn't lost his flair. He's wearing cocoa brown pajamas, a pair of checked boxer shorts on the outside of the bottoms, spotless white crew socks, black Totes slippers, and a hand towel wrapped around his neck like an ascot. With his angular cheekbones and thatch of silvering hair, he might be Samuel Beckett, if Samuel Beckett had been the son of a coal miner from Youngstown, Ohio, an ex-rodeo rider, and a former Skid Row drunk.

Fred has a good heart. On the outside, he's always giving a few bucks to someone in need: a struggling drunk; a down-and-out prostitute (especially if there's a chance she'll sleep with him). In here, he's taken a special liking to one of his three roommates: helping the poor man (he weighs over three hundred pounds) with his slippers, jumping up to whisk away straws and stray bits of plastic—Jell-O lids, syringe wrappings—from beneath his bed. "Thanks for coming by, angel," he says before I've even sat down. "You help me so much."

But what with the abusive childhood, his tour in 'Nam, and the years of drinking, he can also be just a bit of a loose cannon, and I can never tell when he'll snap or come out fighting. He's turned on me before for no reason. He's given me the silent treatment.

In the time that I've known him, I've shown up in spite of myself and often against my better judgment. I've had Fred over for holidays. I've sat by his hospital bed, where he lay unconscious, and prayed. I've dragged myself over to visit him when I'm exhausted, when I feel I should be writing, when I'm hungry, stressed, and lonely. *Is this healthy?* I've thought and, especially after my divorce: *Shouldn't I be on Match.com looking for a boyfriend?* Fred's mellowed of late, or perhaps bowed to providence, but he can still be ornery. "Come sit beside me, sweetie," he'll say, patting the bed, and a minute later, edgily, "Ya mind moving your leg, pal?" "Bring me a bag of M&Ms next time ya come, couldja, just the regular kind, no peanuts." Our "connection" is so tenuous it often seems to have disappeared or gone underground, only to resurface in some tiny moment or glimpse that can't be planned for, asked for, expected, demanded, or, once it's happened, held onto.

I can never figure out whether Fred is hustling me or whether he "gets" me in a way no one else ever quite has or will. I waver between thinking that I'm at least trying to follow "Whatever you did for the least of these brothers of mine, you did for me," and that I'm an A-1 chump. But the kicker was the time a few months ago when he asked me to bring him two Kit-Kats and—selfish, thoughtless oaf that I am—I purchased an eight-pack, drove across town on a sweltering Saturday afternoon, and delivered those instead.

"I said two, not eight," he groused. "That's so alcoholic! If one's good, five is better."

"Good to see you, too," I told him, turned on my heel, and left.

That is it, I thought. *I need to learn how to make a boundary. I need to get rid of the dead wood in my life.* So the next day I fired off a little note. "Where were you when I had cancer?" I ranted. "When have you ever picked me up? When have you ever gone out of your way? I've done a thousand things for you, and in all the years we've known each other, you've done about two for me."

There, I thought, *I've finally washed my hands of that conniving ingrate.* I fully expected him to strike back in the rattlesnake fashion to which I'd become accustomed.

A few days later he called. "I'm sorry you feel that way. I hope we get a chance to talk soon."

That was when I realized Fred filled some strange, no doubt shameful, lack in me and I filled some strange lack in him. That was when I realized I was in for the long haul. That was when I moved one giant step farther toward accepting my complete inability to change another person and my complete inability to change myself. Love has been called many things, but maybe one definition would be the utterly unbridgeable gap between any two humans and the attempt to bridge it anyway.

And so, and yet—here we are. Fred, finished with his breathing treatment, is stretched out on his bed; I'm perched on the edge of his motorized wheelchair, and the Southern California sun, streaming through the chintzy curtains, bathes the scene in a Vermeer-like light. He's still his old self: feisty, philosophical: "Do a little good deed, help your neighbor." But he's fading. He's confused about whether it's Tuesday or Wednesday. He's developed a strange habit of drifting, mid-conversation, from the first person to the third: "You're gonna need a CAT scan, pal," he remarks: I look around to see if someone else has entered the room but no, there's just me.

"Don't you mean *you'll* need a CAT scan?" I ask, but he's already segued, as he also sometimes does now, into delivering his own eulogy. "Yup, old Freddie was a warrior," he says, gazing off toward the San Gabriels with a wry little smile. "Everybody knew and loved Freddie. He always had that certain something about him. He suffered a lot but he bore his suffering bravely, and he never lost his spirit."

"Can it, will you?" I say, but the truth is another spirit would have long ago collapsed from despair, or bitterness, or exhaustion. His spirit is both why he has suffered so much, and why he's survived. His spirit is his glory and his cross, and if I've given him a lot, I've come to see that he gives me a lot, too. He knows I'm not as nice as I like to make myself out to be, nor as self-assured. He accepts me the way I am: my tendency to focus on the unattainable, my sappiness; the way, today, I start talking about God.

I talk about God because I don't know any other way to articulate my holy longing, the anguish of my heart, my knowledge that he's dying. An escaped tear trickles down my cheek; he ignores me. I grope to articulate the mystery of our connection, of existence; he acknowledges me without engaging or much responding, which is really all I want.

I don't know what it is in Fred that invites or allows this level of trust. He often seems hardly to be paying attention (though, weeks after telling him a story, he'll often mention some arcane detail—"That's your Japanese sister-in-law, right, the one who's married to the punk rocker?"— that makes me realize he's been listening all along). Maybe illness is the great leveler. Maybe in silence we share the wounds that are too deep to ever fully heal.

All I know is that I've allowed myself, felt safe enough, to express myself this way with so few people in my life that for a second—even though he's now laying out his pills, nervously fingering, rearranging, turning them one way, then the next, the blue first, the yellow first, all three vertical, then all three horizontal, until it's all I can do not to slap his hand, grab the pills and gulp them down myself—I almost stop breathing.

The preciousness of creatures. That in spite of our fear, our anguish, we're alive. A breath between forgiveness and resentment, distance and closeness, silence and speech. An eye blink between fear and faith, the ridiculous and the sublime, life and death. A razor's edge between the wall that separates and the wall that links: *metaxu*, Simone Weil called this phenomenon, borrowing from Plato: the absence that is also a presence.

Some days when I get up to go Fred says, "Please stay. Please don't leave yet." This afternoon, though, he's ready: dinner at 4:30; *MacNeil-Lehrer* at 6:00. In his collarless pajamas, he's like some exquisite, wasted mandarin, on the last days of his throne.

"Thanks, angel, you're so good to me. When d'ya think you can make it out again?" he asks.

"Coupla weeks maybe." Then—I'm musing—"Sometimes I wonder why we don't all kill ourselves. What holds us back—some moment in our childhoods, maybe? Some summer afternoon, some boy, some girl…"

He hacks, examines his handkerchief.

"Naw, that's not what keeps me going," he waves me off. "What keeps me going, tell ya the truth—I just wanna be around to see what crazy thing happens next."

* * *

What happened next was not, as it turned out, great. During visits, he started saying, "I'm not gonna make it, Heather, I'm never going home." He began referring to "the hereafter." He kept bugging me about a will, so I downloaded one from online, rounded up another witness, and brought it in. "Household Effects," "Cash," and "All Other Assets" would go to his brother Rann, his one relative, back in Ohio: signed Alfred Leroy Davis III.

I thought of his bachelor apartment with the smoke-stained walls, the bills lined up in military rows on the dresser, the packets of ketchup from Taco Bell in the fridge, the pinup rodeo girl tacked to the wall of his closet, the paper lunch bag on the floor by the bed filled with spent cigarette butts, his drawer with the SSI checks that had been accumulating, because he's been at the VA for over a year now.

He started to fail in earnest. Rann flew in. I picked him up at LAX—we'd never met—and then I picked him up the next day at his hotel and brought him to the VA where I got to see him and Fred greet each other for the first time (and what would be the last time, ever) in ten years. I began to fear that Fred would die when I was out of town. Headed to the airport one night for a red-eye to Boston, I stopped by the hospital first. We watched the sun set together, and he gave me his peanut-butter-and-jelly sandwich for the plane.

He was in and out of intensive care, and finally, he was in for good. One morning I drove over and they had him in a glassed-in contamination pod. I could see him in there: tied down, his hands bandaged mitts.

"You're not taking that bottle of water," the nurse said. I threw out the water.

"Put on that mask." I put on the mask.

"Don't touch him." I won't touch him.

"Don't wake him up." I won't wake him up.

Finally I went in. He looked like Christ on the cross: sweating, bruised. His hair was plastered to his forehead, he was in restraints and on a vent, and his arms, from where he'd tried to tear out the needles, looked like someone had gone over them with a sledge-hammer. I stood against the far wall, saying Hail Marys, whispering, "Dear Jesus, Freddie, this is bad. It's Heather, Freddie. I'm right here with you." Two minutes later the nurse came along with an entourage of underlings and kicked me out, saying she had to draw blood.

I stood outside the door for a half hour and the next time she came out I said, "I'm wondering when I can go back in and see my friend."

"Oh no, no, no," she preened, "you work around us. We can't just…"

"You are an *idiot*," I hissed. I was shaking. I could feel the muscles in my face contorting in scary, tic-like ways I was glad I couldn't see. "That is not a patient to me; that is my friend. He has been suffering for years, and he is freaking *dying*. All I wanted was to touch his hand. All I wanted was to tell him he is loved. Do you not get that is a human being in there? Do you not get that he is dying?"

She flinched, and I was glad. I had wanted to wound her and I'd succeeded. I broke my lifelong never-sic-management-on-a-lowly-worker rule and called her manager the next day, too, and I didn't feel one bit sorry.

They put him on palliative care, with nature scenes continuously looping on the overhead TV. I got my friend Father Terry to come in, not so much as a priest, but as a human being and a sober alcoholic. Fred had no use for Jesus, so even though we weren't sure he even knew we were there, we didn't bring Jesus up. We touched his arm and held his hand and said how grateful we were that we'd all gotten sober; and that we'd be with him, whatever happened; and that we hoped to see him again someday. So little (though so good of Fr. Terry), but I'd wanted to establish some link with the eternal; to let the universe know that someone had cared about the state of Fred's soul.

September 7, 2009, was Monday of the Labor Day weekend. I rarely allow myself a Monday of any kind off, but a friend asked me to have coffee that morning and I said, "OK, let's." We went to LAMill, a pretentious, ridiculously overpriced coffee boutique on Silver Lake Boulevard. Afterward, I thought of going to see Fred but I was wiped out and the sun was beating down and instead I came home and lay down with a book. I didn't have a good feeling.

Later that afternoon Rann called. "Freddie's gone," he said, but somehow I'd already known. Twenty years, and as Fred breathed his last I'd been drinking a six-dollar cup of Organic Black Onyx at an "artsy-fartsy" café.

Right away, though, I knew that wasn't what I wanted to remember. I could have felt bad that I wasn't at Fred's side, but I chose to feel grateful I'd ever shown up at all. I could have focused on his terrible pain, but I chose to realize that because I'd been in pain myself, we'd been able to share our loneliness.

You have to be in simply unbelievable pain to sit in silence with another person; to endure that level of ineffectiveness, of poverty. Who but someone as fearful of getting close as Fred was could have put up with Fred? Who but someone confused about the line between service and self-neglect could have meshed so thoroughly with someone so confused about the line between gratitude and manipulation? Fred died alone, but I chose to enshrine in memory an exchange that may qualify as my/our/the über metaxu moment:

A year ago, just before Christmas, I'd flown East for the holidays. Several days later, Rann had called to report that Fred had suffered the umpteenth medical crisis and been rushed yet again to ICU. Things didn't look good. So when I returned to Los Angeles, I went over the very next morning to the VA.

Fred was always at least marginally glad to see me, but when I walked into the room this time his face lit up as if my very existence were an epiphany, and he started saying the kinds of things he'd never said before.

"I've always, always loved you, Heather. You'll never know how much."

"Well, I've always loved you, too."

"No, but I mean really loved. I kept testing you, but you always came back. I tried to push you away but you never left. I'm so screwed up I didn't know how to show it, but sometimes I even wanted to give you a little kiss..."

"Oh Fred," I said, taking his hand, "that is so sweet. We always have had some strange kind of bond. Not romantic of course, but..."

"Ya never know," he interrupted. "Maybe when I get out of here..."

He must know time is growing short, I thought fondly. *He must finally want me to know how special I've been to him. Sure he was a little morphined out, but this puts things on a whole new footing. Finally, he's gonna quit this hot-cold stuff. Finally, we're going to start communicating. Finally, we're going to have a real friendship.*

A couple of days later he called. "That was so nice, our talk Saturday," I said a little shyly. "That's probably the nicest talk we've ever had."

There was a pause, as if, in some other, unimaginably distant realm, a blind man were groping, helplessly, hopelessly along a wall for a nonexistent door.

"You were in Saturday?" he asked.

Chapter Eighteen

PERSEVERANCE

Paradise Found

There are nothing but gifts on this poor, poor Earth.[1]
—Czeslaw Milosz

Soon after being confirmed, I worked up the courage to quit my
job at the law firm where I'd worked for three years and start
writing. I'd been terrified of giving up my salary, but following
my passion for the first time in my life was its own kind of abundance. Discipline was a gift, perseverance a blessing. Day by day I
learned about my shortcomings, and about my strengths. I learned
that writing is a craft, and there is no way to get better except
by practice. I'd found my calling at last, and after a while I was
unable to tell whether I was creating the writing or the writing
was creating me.

Still, I'd given up a lot of money. Consumed by financial
worries, I would ponder the parables of the lost coin and the fallen
sparrow. The crowds crying, "Crucify him! Crucify him!" in the
passion story emblemized the violence of trying to make things
the way I want them to be instead of accepting them as they are.
"And the meek shall inherit the earth" reminded me that there is
no more powerful act in the world than one human being saying
to another, "I was wrong," or, "I care about you."

Christ knew all about caring. He knew that one of the saddest
things we have to live with on this earth is our loneliness, our

sense of expulsion and exile. He knew that when you really love someone, you want to devour them, to become one with them, and you can't do that with another human being. So he did it in the Eucharist.

Dorothy Day, that great Catholic anarchist who championed the poor all her life, said, "We cannot love God unless we love each other, and to love we must know each other. We know Him in the breaking of bread."[2] I'm lucky enough to live in a city that offers Mass morning, noon and night, and I go as often as I can. I want richness of experience, like-minded people, a certain sensibility, but things are seldom the way *I* want them. Sometimes I end up going to a strange church, because I'm always rushing around in a frenzy, afraid I won't be able to keep up, that I'll be left behind.

One recent Sunday, I was hurrying to make it to afternoon Mass at an unfamiliar church. Instead of resting, as Christ suggested, I'd spent the day driving the Pasadena freeway in the broiling sun, then looking for a parking space, then shopping at Target, and then standing in line with my purchases. Now I was back in the car with an iced coffee, which I somehow managed to spill all over my pants, and I was going to be late for a five o'clock Mass.

Why was everything always so hard?

I walked into this hot, unfamiliar, crowded white-bread church. The Mass was horrible: the lame guitars, the syrupy singing, the people who came late and squeezed in next to me, the kid crying in the next pew, the smarmy Irish priest. Is there anything more depressing than a guitar Mass and a female cantor who sounds like Karen Carpenter? Plus they had this cornball practice of not only holding hands during the Lord's Prayer, which was bad enough, but scooching over and holding hands across the pews. I was convinced: nobody there felt as lost and awful as me. No, they were all enjoying it. They liked the crappy music. They'd all gotten their lives together and found people to marry and were raising well-adjusted children. I was tired and cranky and afraid, and I'd been alone all day. I'd been alone, whether through temperament or choice, most of my life.

Finally we got to the Eucharist, and while I was standing in line with my bitten-down fingernails and coffee-stained pants, it suddenly struck me that this teenager holding a chintzy gold bowl of Communion wafers was doing the two things I'd been subconsciously longing for someone to do all day: he was acknowledging me as a human being, and he was giving me a gift—and not just any gift, but the Body of Christ.

"The Body of Christ," said the acne-scarred boy, his patient eyes on mine, and all the crankiness and fear drained out of me. He didn't do this because I was special. (He'd done it for everyone else too.) He did it simply because I came. "I know my sheep, and my sheep know me," Christ said. I hadn't been forgotten after all. We'd found each other, there in the pasture.

* * *

Christ knew all about hunger, so much so that he gave us his very body to eat. He consented to become what is basically the hardest thing in the world to be: a mortal human being. He ate among us, sat around, told jokes with us. Like most of us, he was not loved enough, noticed enough, appreciated enough. He didn't get the girl. He was lonely, misunderstood, slandered, betrayed, and saw his life's work seemingly go for naught. Christ embodied and lived the sum total of what I've learned in life, which is that the truth about things is hidden, it is small, and it is scorned and mocked by the world. Out of this poverty and want, this failure and humiliation, he created a temple "not made by human hands" to fulfill the deepest desire of every human heart, which is not to be so eternally, everlastingly alone.

I believe the Eucharist is the true Body and the true Blood because my heart has been turned, more than once, from stone to flesh; because I've been forgiven and I've forgiven others; because for a drunk to get sober is more miraculous than the moving of any mountain. I believe it because the bread of our daily lives— the least remarkable of our experiences, the least among us, the least loveable, least understandable parts of ourselves—seems to be exactly where we are most likely to meet God.

Catholics are required to be obedient, a fact that doesn't sit well with many "independent" thinkers. I've never had much trouble with the outward obediences. I go to Mass every Sunday and most days during the week. I go to confession, though not as often as I could or probably should. When I was married, I didn't use artificial birth control, and when I was divorced, I got an annulment.

But I'm not blindly, stupidly obedient. Nor am I too lazy or afraid to think for myself. I'm obedient because I was obedient to myself for most of my life, and it was a disaster. "Take up your cross and follow me," Jesus said, but he also said, "My yoke is easy, my burden light." If taking up my own little cross—basically, looking at myself and trying to change for the better— has sometimes been painful and lonely, it hasn't been nearly as painful and lonely as when I was out there exercising my "freedom."

As Dorothy Day observed and Romano Guardini said, "The Church is the Cross upon which Christ was crucified...and one must live in a state of permanent dissatisfaction with the

Church."[3] But I, for one, am glad the Church doesn't try to please everybody. Whatever its failings, it's the only organization I know that's for life across the board: against both capital punishment and abortion, euthanasia and nuclear weapons. These positions grant life, and the sex that gives rise to it, the sacramental position it deserves.

The time may be coming for the Church to die and rise again in some form we can't yet imagine. In the meantime, I can hardly expect an institution comprised of fallen humans to be anything but fallen itself. There is no way to be washed clean of that bone-deep shame, guilt, and sorrow except to be baptized with fire and water, to be born again, to become a "new creation" through Christ (2 Corinthians 5:17).

The Church is often seen as a bastion of conservatism, a power-based hierarchy. But Christ subverted all power systems: political, cultural, personal. There is no braver, more difficult, or more radical act of countercultural resistance than giving with no expectation of return; than learning, as St. Francis of Assisi did, that it is better to comfort than to be comforted. We're the ones who devised a world based on rewards and punishments. Christ preached a very different kind of world, one based not on what we deserve—for none of us *deserve* anything—but on love.

Jesus knew that true love, and therefore true transformation, takes place in the face-to-face encounter. Feeling love for victims of a natural disaster halfway around the world is easier than loving the neighbor whose music disturbs your sleep, or the meter maid who's just given you a ticket, or the spouse who just ruined your best pair of jeans when you told him not to use bleach. These are tasks requiring superhuman help.

Catholicism has a wealth of ritual: the liturgy, the feasts, the saints; the annual cycle of Advent, Lent, and Ordinary Time. I've observed these long enough that they've begun to order my days, my years, my psyche. Almost every morning I pray the Divine Office, with its psalms, canticles, responses, and readings, and at night I attempt at least a brief examination of conscience.

Rich as all this is, I can't say I've been transformed by it—at least, not in any way I'd hoped to be. My prayers are often frustrated: "I'm no good, I hate everybody, and all I think about is sex." I spend entire Masses hunched over and sobbing. I once knelt in the confessional and admitted that I was prideful, slothful, selfish, judgmental, rageful, and rude. There was a long pause, after which the priest asked, "Are you a very unhappy person?"

"Oh, no!" I replied hastily, committing yet another sin: lying. Although I'm not really unhappy. I just seldom have a good time.

More and more I see the wisdom of St. Thérèse of Lisieux's "Little Way." To pray not only for the people I love, but for those who have wronged me, threatened me, disturbed me. To give a portion of what little extra money I have to someone who needs it more. To give thanks at the end of the day, for a thousand more things have gone right, always, than have gone wrong. These practices don't seem like much, but I have to believe they change the world in a way we're not given to see. I don't have any remarkable skills. I am not patient or generous. But I can answer phone calls, show up on time, drive, and tell a joke or two—all you need, really, to perform acts of mercy.

"You just want some comfort," agnostics sometimes jeer at believers. "You just want some consolation." I can hardly fathom the mean-spiritedness that would deny a drop of consolation to a brother or sister in anguish. In this world where there's nowhere to lay your head, no answers, no fixes, quick or otherwise, I, for one, wish we could all have *more* consolation—and I think Jesus, who in his anguish sweated tears of blood in the Garden of Gethsemane the night before he died, wishes that for us, too.

In my own anxiety and loneliness, I imagine sitting with him in the garden, or standing along the Via Dolorosa as he passes by carrying the cross. In happier moods, I tell him, "Isn't it nice to have clean sheets, Jesus?" or "Look at that ruby-throated hummingbird, Lord. Isn't it beautiful!" And however poor my progress or halting my discipleship, prayer and the sacraments have given me Jesus as a Real, True Friend.

The other day I was taking a walk through my economically depressed neighborhood—the dog crap and the noisy kids and the ice-cream trucks and the sun shining and the scraggly pink oleanders blooming in the overgrown lot—when I suddenly experienced a feeling of incredible certainty that it is all right, that it is all here, and that it is all so incredibly beautiful that I could have fallen to my knees on the oil-stained sidewalk and wept.

Jesus tells the parable of a merchant who searches far and wide for the world's most precious pearl. When he finds the jewel, the merchant sees that it will cost him everything he owns, but he buys it anyway.

My poverty of spirit continues, but a moment like the one I had on my walk—I'd sell everything for it. It was the pearl of great price that's worth a whole life.

Notes

CHAPTER ONE

1. McKenzie Wark, "There is another world, and it is this one," Public Seminar, http://www.publicseminar.org/2014/01/there—is—another—world—and—it—is—this—one/#.U7Q6WPldWSo.

2. Flannery O' Connor, letter dated July 20, 1955, in *The Habit of Being: Letters of Flannery O'Connor*, Sally Fitzgerald, ed. (New York: Farrar, Straus and Giroux, 1988), p. 90.

3. John Donne, "Batter my heart, three-person'd God," quoted in Philip Zaleski and Carol Zaleski, *Prayer: A History* (New York: Mariner Books, 2006), p. 279.

4. Gerard Manley Hopkins, "God's Grandeur," quoted in Graham Storey, *A Preface to Hopkins* (London: Longman Group, 1992), p. 73.

5. Quoted at Deborah J. Brasket, "More on 'The Writing Life' with Annie Dillard," Living on the Edge of the Wild blog, http://deborahbrasket.wordpress.com/2014/08/28/more-on-the-writing-life-with-annie-dillard/. Retrieved on August 28, 2014.

CHAPTER THREE

1. See Søren Kierkegaard, *Purity of Heart Is to Will One Thing* (Radford, Va.: Wilder, 2008).

2. Dorothy Day, *The Duty of Delight: The Diaries of Dorothy Day*, ed. Robert Ellsberg (New York: Doubleday, 2011), p. 202.

3. Day, p. xix.

4. Day, p. xv.

5. Day, p. 73.

6. Day, p. 90.

7. Day, p. 64.

8. Day, p. 530.

9. Day, p. 71.

10. Day, p. 560.

11. Day, p. 359.

12. Day, p. 54.

13. Day, p. 638.

14. Day, p. 166.

15. Day, p. 540.
16. Day, p. 540.
17. Day, p. 459.

CHAPTER FIVE

1. O'Connor, *Habit of Being*, p. 126
2. Daniel Weiss, "The New Normal? — Youth Exposure to Online Pornography," Citizen Link, January 27, 2012, http://www.citizenlink.com/2012/01/27/the—new—normal—%E2%80%93—youth—exposure—to—online—pornography/.
3. O'Connor, *Habit of Being*, p. 117.
4. Quoted in John Ortberg, *Love Beyond Reason* (New York: HarperCollins, 2010).
5. Caryll Houselander, *Mother of Christ* (London: Sheed and Ward, 1978), p. 64.
6. Quoted in Philip Yancey, *What's So Amazing about Grace?* (Grand Rapids: Zondervan, 1997).
7. Romano Guardini, *The Lord* (Washington, D.C.: Regnery, 2000), p. 426.
8. Carlos Drummond de Andrade, "Souvenir…," quoted at http://wiz.cath.vt.edu/pipermail/new—poetry/2003—February/021992.html.

CHAPTER SIX

1. Quoted in Mel Williams, "Searching for What We Already Have," Watts Street Baptist Church, March 7, 2011, http://www.wattsstreet.org/mod/news/print.php?article_id=2358.
2. Margaret Wertheim, *The Pearly Gates of Cyberspace: A History of Space from Dante to the Internet* (New York: Norton, 2000), p. 210.

CHAPTER SEVEN

1. Gerald G. May, *The Dark Night of the Soul* (New York: HarperCollins, 2009), pp. 72–73, quoting John of the Cross, *Dark Night of the Soul*, book 1, chapter 9.7.
2. Ron Rolheiser, O.M.I., "Celibacy as Solidarity with the Poor," Ron Rolheiser blog, June 14, 1995, http://ronrolheiser.com/celibacy—as—solidarity—with—the—poor/#.VAEYefkwem4.
3. Walker Percy, "Walker Percy Interviews Himself," Bad Catholic blog, http://www.patheos.com/blogs/badcatholic/2011/11/walker-percy-interviews-himself.html.

4. O'Connor, *Habit of Being*, p. 93
5. Robert Zaretsky, *A Life Worth Living: Albert Camus and the Quest for Meaning* (Cambridge, Ma.: Belknap, 2013), p. 90.

CHAPTER EIGHT

1. Frederick Buechner, "The Longing for Home," http://m. frederickbuechner.com/content/longing—home—page—137.

CHAPTER ELEVEN

1. Thomas Merton, "House of Prayer, The. Notes," The Thomas Merton Center at Bellarmine University, http://www.merton.org/research/ Manuscripts/manu.aspx?id=2930.
2. Madeleine L'Engle, *Walking on Water: Reflections on Faith and Art* (Wheaton, Ill.: Harold Shaw, 1980), p. 122.
3. Quoted in Joseph F. Schmidt, F.S.C., *Walking the Little Way of Thérèse of Lisieux: Discovering the Path of Love* (Frederick, Md.: Word Among Us, 2012).

CHAPTER SIXTEEN

1. Christopher Hitchens, "Mommie Dearest: The pope beatifies Mother Teresa, a fanatic, a fundamentalist, and a fraud," *Slate*, October 20, 2003, http://www.slate.com/articles/news_and_politics/fighting_ words/2003/10/mommie_dearest.html.

CHAPTER SEVENTEEN

1. Quoted in *Christianity and Western Thought*, vol. 3 (Downers Grove, Ill.: InterVarsity, 2009), p. 125.

CHAPTER EIGHTEEN

1. Czeslaw Milosz, "The Separate Notebooks," quoted in Edward Hirsch, *Poet's Choice* (New York: Harcourt, 2006), p. 98.
2. Dorothy Day, *The Long Loneliness The Autobiography of the Legendary Catholic Social Activist* (San Francisco: HarperOne, 2009), p. 285.
3. Kenneth L. Woodward, *Making Saints: How The Catholic Church Determines Who Becomes a Saint* (New York: Touchstone, 1996), p. 30.

ABOUT THE AUTHOR

Heather King is the author of *Parched; Redeemed; Shirt of Flame; Poor Baby;* and *Stripped: Cancer, Culture and the Cloud of Unknowing.* She lives in Los Angeles, speaks nationwide, contributes regularly to *Magnificat,* and is a popular blogger.